TEACHING TECHNIQUES

TEACHING TECHNIQUES

Dr. R.S.S. Nehru

M.Sc., M.S.W., M.Sc., M.Ed., M.Phil., Ph.D.,
Reader in Education
Benniah Christian College of Education
Rajahmundry,
Andhra Pradesh.

A P H PUBLISHING CORPORATION
4435-36/7, ANSARI ROAD, DARYA GANJ
NEW DELHI-110 002

Published by
S.B. Nangia
A.P.H. Publishing Corporation
4435–36/7, Ansari Road, Darya Ganj,
New Delhi-110002
Phone: 011–23274050
e-mail: aphbooks@gmail.com

2026

Rs. 2495/-

Typeset by
Ideal Publishing Solutions
C-90, J.D. Cambridge School,
West Vinod Nagar, Delhi-110092

Printed at
RD DIGITAL PRINTERS
Ansari road , Daryaganj, Delhi-110002

PREFACE

Educational objectives have been classified and defined in terms of cognitive, affective and psychomotor outcomes. While much of the large volume of knowledge acquired year after year might be forgotten soon, the affective outcomes have better prospects greater stability over time, like cognitive and psychomotor capabilities. Like values, attitudes have a prominent place among the affective outcomes; they represent two levels in a hierarchy. Development of healthy, sound attitudes is an important component of the total function of the school and of any general education programme.

It is said that today's children are tomorrow's citizen's. In the present context, we see that young students often have misguided notions and feelings about social phenomena and issues. It is the duty of all concerned, especially of the educators, to set the notions and attitudes right, in order to achieve a cohesive, peaceful and productive society. Then only happy and harmonious socializing can be possible. This necessitates the development and for changing of many socially relevant attitudes.

Certain attitudes assume special relevance and demand urgent attention in a society in a given period. Formation and change of such attitudes, becomes the concern of the society as a whole and of education, in particular. In the present Indian context, attitudes in respect of Casteism, family planning, manual work, dowry system, corruption in public life, environmental pollution, village setting and rural life, etc., seem to be of special importance.

According to common observations our, society is increasingly plagued by caste considerations, by bias and prejudice, divisions and preferences, alliances and allegations based on caste, despite our avowed faith in and commitment to equality, fraternity, secularism and socialism. Similarly, our planned and concerted efforts for improving living conditions, raising the standard and quality of life, providing suitable employment opportunities to all and doing so many other things that would contribute to the establishment of a truly welfare society on firm footing are said to be offset by the 'population explosion'. Intensive and extensive population education has been suggested as a key solution need for earnest population control. Small family norms and family planning for better life for all, hoped that if they are provided to be productive, they could be employed on a wider scale and has been emphasized and such message, propagated in so many ways for the last many years. Still the population growth has not been arrested. The problems of unemployment and underemployment is staggering inspire of emphasis on and previous for job oriented education, vocational education, self employment, etc., academic course and specializations, university degrees and white collar jobs continue to have prestige and to attract people's fancies and preferences, the dignity of labour is emphasized in theory and in profession, but manual work continues to be looked down upon by many. Much can be said on these liens about the other attitudes mentioned above. Thus, the need for attempting to change certain attitudes of students in the right direction and studying certain Teaching Techniques that seems to hold promise of reasonable effect in the normal school setting. Also it was thought that the retentively of the induced attitude change is of latest interest.

The experimental treatments in this project were conceived, planned and organized within a framework of strengths and weaknesses - with limitations inherent in the investigation any one person for that matter. The human and material resources he could master though he tried to do his best in this regard and the situation involvement of outside personnel, as communicators, student perception of the programme as extracurricular activities, time for the session and the spread of the programme, organizational facilities, made available to an outside agency, etc.

There is scope simple scope for improvement in the planning, materials production, and organization phases of the programme. It would only be reasonable then, to expect that better programme would yield higher gains, and all the strategies and activities tried out are very suitable for normal school, college setting and programmes as curricular or co-curricular activities; they have also been found to be quite productive and promising.

They have to be planned and organized on a wider scale in all schools and colleges. Teachers/Teacher educators have to be prepared for this role of change agents in respect of healthy social attitudes through well-conceived and adequate components in the pre-service and in-service teacher training. It would also be advantageous to us to produce materials of all kinds required for such programmes in a centralized way. So, if the school system accepts the development of healthy social attitudes and production of significant changes in them in desired direction, as an important part of its function, it could - and should - plan and organize such activities in a concerted way as an integral part of its total programme and that should make education more interesting and more socially relevant and useful.

ACKNOWLEDGEMENTS

I express my sincere, respectful and unforgettable gratitude to my preceptor and task master Dr. Nimma Venkata Rao, Professor and Dean Faculty of Education, Department of Education, Andhra University, whose inspiring guidance, constant supervision and constructive suggestions have been of invaluable help to me in completing this piece of research without which it would not have seen the light.

I take this opportunity to place on record my deep sense of gratitude to Prof. Y. Bhaskaracharayulu, Department of Education (Merged), Andhra University, Visakhapatnam for providing me an opportunity to fulfill my ambition for his valuable guidance throughout my career.

My sincere thanks to Dr. P.S. Rao, Wng. Cdr. (IAF) for his encouragement and support for completion of my research work.

My Sincere thanks to all the other Governmental agencies and schools which were very considerate in going out of their way to help me to make the programme a success.

Last but not least I am grateful to my all family members, my wife Smt. Usha and my beloved twins Chy. Sai Sailesh and Chy. Sai Sarath (Adi) for all the credit of my success from whom I drew my inspiration and strength to carry on the research work till its completion. They are my supporters who encouraged me throughout my research work I owe to them immensely for their patience, love and encouragement throughout my Research.

Ravipalli Sri Santhi Nehru

CONTENTS

LIST OF TABLES

LIST OF FIGURES

ABBREVIATIONS

BC	Backward Caste
CD – ROM	Compact Disk Read Only Memory
DVD	Digital Versatile Disk
et al.	and others
ICT	Integrated Communication Technology
OC	Other Caste
SC	Scheduled Caste
SES	Socio-Economic Status
ST	Scheduled Tribe
T_1	Verbal-visual communication strategy
T_2	Dramatized multimedia communication strategy
T_3	Integrated (t_1–t_2) communication strategy
TV	Television
VISAC	Visakha Student Attitude Toward Casteism
VISAF	Visakha Student Attitude Toward Family Planning
VISAM	Visakha Student Attitude Toward Manual Work

About the Book

Teaching Techniques – An experimental study refers to attitudes form not only colorful determinants of behavior but also an absorbing area of research. Attitudes are stable mental dispositions towards psychological objects such as persons, ideas, objects, institutions and situations in the environment formed basing on one's experiences and having cognitive, affective and psychomotor domains. They may be positive (favorable) or negative (unfavorable) with variations in strength that can be represented on a dichotomous continuum.

Attitudes also form a major set of relatively stable affective outcomes of education. Developing healthy attitudes or producing attitude change in the right direction is a part of the function of education. Therefore, psychologists, sociologists and educationalists should be interested not only in assessing attitudes as they are in a given individual or group but also in the factors and procedures those facilitate attitude formation and change. Certain attitudes assume special relevance in a society in a given period. Formation or change of such attitudes, then, becomes the concern of the society in general and on education in particular. In the present Indian context, attitudes in respect of family planning, Casteism and manual work among other things seem to be of special importance. Theories of attitudinal change and a wide range of studies on attitudes especially attitude changes have been reviewed.

Educational objectives have been classified and defined in terms of cognitive, affective and psychomotor outcomes. While much of the large volume of knowledge acquired year after year might be forgotten soon, the affective outcomes have better prospects greater stability over time like cognitive and psychomotor capabilities. Like values, attitudes have a prominent place among the affective outcomes; they represent two levels in a hierarchy. Development of healthy, sound attitudes is an important component of the total function of the school and of any general education programme.

The independent variables are the different Teaching Strategies employed in effecting attitudinal change and it took three treatment forms as mentioned above, while the three attitudes those towards Manual Work, Casteism and Family Planning formed the dependent variables. Other variables like time interval, essential content and length of the treatment and source were controlled by making them uniform for all the groups, so that the effect of variables become neutral. The recipient variables were also adequately controlled by systematic sampling technique and a rotation design. Sex and SES were taken as predictor variables in relation to the criteria of initial position and changes achieved in respect of dependent variables and those are attitudes.

The study was conceived as an experimental study aimed at finding the effectiveness of the three treatments, viz., verbal –visual communication methods (T_1), dramatized-multimedia methods (T_2) and Integrated of these two methods (T_3), in producing change in the desired direction in three attitudes of the students studying IX class in Secondary Schools. It also aimed at finding the differences by sex and socio-economic status (SES), religion, rural, urban in respect of the initial position on the three attitudes and changes achieved in them through the treatment.

This Book is framed keeping in the mind of the above mentioned Teaching Strategies, Author was very much pertinent with the abreast of latest information regarding the Developmental line of Teaching Strategies, methods and pedagogy principles and practice in the view of Indian school and college setting. He has to be planned and organized for wider scale in all schools, colleges, teacher training colleges and behaviour trainees also. Teachers/Teacher educators have to be prepared for this role of change agents in respect of healthy social attitudes through well-conceived and adequate components in the pre-service, in-service teacher training and management trainees also. It would also be advantage to us to produce materials of all kinds required for such programmes in a centralized way. So, if the school system accepts the development of healthy social attitudes and production of significant changes in them in desired direction, as an important part of its function, it could - and should plan and organize such activities in a concerted way as an integral part of its total programme and that should make education more interesting and more socially relevant and useful.

About the Author

Dr. Ravipalli Sri Santhi Nehru is presently Reader, Benniah Christian College of Education, P.G. Department, Rajahmundry, Andhra Pradesh. He is also Consultant in Education and Management. He is Research Director for M.Phil., and Ph.D. programme. He has Master Degrees Educational Qualifications such as in M.Sc. (Zoology)., M.S.W., M.Sc. (Psychology)., M.Ed., M.Phil. (Education), Ph.D. (Education), PGDHR, PGDCA.

He has been teaching under graduate and post graduate students since from 2002. He has published 8 Books and 8 Research Articles in the National Journals. Presented 30 Thematic and Research Papers in National and International Conferences. He attended 7 workshops and 5 symposia. His areas of Interest are research in Educational Technology, Educational Psychology, Teacher Education with inter disciplinary.

Email: dr.rssnehru@gmail.com

CHAPTER 1

INTRODUCTION

Attitudes are usually defined as a disposition or tendency to respond positively or negatively towards a certain things like idea, object, person and situation. Attitudes are encompassed or closely related to our opinions and beliefs and are based upon our experiences. Since attitudes often relate in some way to interact with others they represent an important link between cognitive and social psychology. As far as instruction is concerned, a great deal of learning involves acquiring or changing attitudes.

An attitude is a hypothetically constructed that represents an individual's like or dislike for an item. Attitudes are positive, negative or neutral views of an "attitudinal object"; i.e. a *person*, a behavioural or an trait event. People can also be "ambivalent" towards a target, meaning that they simultaneously possess a positive and negative bias towards the attitude in question.

1.1 THEORETICAL BACKGROUND

1.1.1 Attitude

Attitudes come from judgments. Attitudes develop on effective response, behavioural change and cognitive response which is called the ABC model. The affective response is a *physiological* response that expresses an individual's preference for an entity. The behavioral change is a verbal indication of the intention of an individual. The cognitive response is a cognitive evaluation of the entity to form an attitude. Most attitudes in individuals are a result of *observational learning* from their environment. The link between the attitude and the existing behavior depends on human behavior some of which are irrational.

A person's attitude represents how he/she feels or his/her state of mind is about something. For example, one can have a good (or positive) attitude towards his work, usually meaning, that he feels good of his job the organization etc., Many features of working in an organization can cause a person to have a poor attitude about their jobs and organizations-that is they feel bad about their jobs and organizations, because of inadequate compensation, conflicts with their supervisor, inconsistent or conflicting communications from the senior management, unfulfilling work, hostile communications between employees etc. Some people adopt a poor attitude because that is their way of being in the world, i.e., they often resent their environment no matter what is going on around them. Some people feel poorly about themselves which affects their attitude about their environment, as well. In contrast, some people work hard to keep a positive attitude. These people often have better overall health and can effectively address major challenges in the workplace, as well.

Attitudes are powerful affective-cognitive forces in man and influence his behavior. In discussing the history of the concept of attitude Mc Guire (1964) noted that it was so central to social psychology that it was often equated with it. Thurstone's (1929) definition of attitude is that, it is a generalized reaction for or against a specific psychological object. The object may be a person or a group, a kind of object or living thing, concept or value, an event or situation, an institution or system. Allport (1935) considered attitude as a "mental and neural state of readiness to respond, organized through experience, exerting a directive and/or dynamic influence on behaviour". According to Krech, Cautchfield and Ballachey (1962 pp. 177) an attitude is "an enduring system of positive or negative evaluation, emotional feelings and pro- or con-action tendencies with respect to a social object".

Thus as man, in his finite world, comes across the same object the repeatedly evoked cognitions, feelings, and response dispositions, become organized into a unified and enduring system which can be called his attitude toward that object".

1.1.2. Nature of attitudes

Attitudes can be thought of as constructs having three kinds of components: cognitive, affective and psychomotor. The cognitive component of an attitude means the knowledge and beliefs of the individual about the psychological object concerned. The most critical cognition incorporated in the attitude system is evaluative beliefs, which involve the attributing of 'favourable' or 'unfavourable', 'good' or 'bad', qualities to an object. The affective component refers to the feelings and emotions connected with the object. An object is felt to be 'liked' or 'disliked', pleasing' or 'displeasing', 'loved' or 'hated'. It is this emotional loading, which gives the attitudes their insistent, stirred up, activating or motivating character. The cognitive component makes for all the behavioral readiness associated with an attitude. If an individual wields a positive attitude towards a given object, he would be disposed to receive, seek, support, reward or serve the object and on the other hand attitude if he holds a negative attitude he would be inclined to avoid, reject, harm, punish or destroy the object.

An attitude is conventionally conceptualized as a single bipolar attribute with 'positive' and 'negative' or 'favorable' and 'unfavorable' directions or sides, meaning thereby that it would not be found simultaneously at both ends of the dimension, though, like 'love-hate relationships' in common parlor, a unified structure and compromised position of positive and negative thoughts and feelings would be possible. A variety of such positional combination along the continuum from extreme positive to extreme negative positions, leads to the concept of a 'neutral attitude' falling in the middle range. The presence of both 'favorable' and 'unfavorable' elements relating to the different features of the same total object in the composite attitude is its 'ambivalence'.

By the term 'intensity' of an attitude, we mean its strength of feeling. 'Salience' of an attitude denotes the readiness with which a person expresses an attitude'. Scott (1960) considered the 'effective salience' of an attitude as the degree to which a person's view of the object is dominated by the evaluative content. The cognitive component of an attitude depends on the cognitive elaboration and structuring of the object in experience and internalization, or the richness of the ideational content. Krech, Crutchfield and Ballachy (1962) called the prominence of the conative component, or 'action tendency' as 'covertness'. An attitude is said to be flexible to the extent to which it may be modified by a variety of pressures. The 'embeddedness' of an attitude is its connectedness with other cognitive structures and attitudes. The total set of attitudes of an individual makes up his attitude 'constellation'.

1.1.3 Development and change of attitudes

Formation and change of attitude are not two separate things, they are interwoven. People are always adopting, modifying, and relinquishing attitudes to fit their ever-changing needs and interests. Attitude cannot be changed by simple education. Acceptance of new attitudes depends on who is presenting the knowledge, how it is presented, how the person is perceived, the credibility of the communicator, and the conditions by which the knowledge was received.

Change of attitude occurs when a person receives new information from others or media, Cognitive change is due to the following:

- Through direct experience with the attitude object–Affective change.
- Force a person to behave in a way different than normal-behavioral change.

An attitude can be changed by a number of sources including other people, family, media, church, or the object itself. In 1968, McGuire developed steps in changing attitudes. The steps are – attention, comprehension, yielding, retention, and action. Triandis (1971) said, "In analyzing the attitude-change process, we must consider the effect of, who says what, how to whom, with what effect.

Attitude can be changed basing on how a person receives the communication and the communicator. Less committed people will change ideas more frequently. Attitude change also has to do with other personality characteristics such as susceptibility to persuasion, intelligence, readiness to accept change, etc. We are more likely to accept information if we feel the communicator has no intent to change our attitudes and opinions.

Attitudes develop through situations and experiences involving the psychological objects concerned that serve to construct various images and concepts, feelings and motions, and behavior patterns. Physical and social contacts and interactions result in the establishment of cognitive structures, conscious or involuntary adjustments and reaction tendencies. The child, born into and reared in a society is continually subjected to ever-changing social stimuli. Socially, he becomes largely what the environment makes him. As Mead (1934) pointed out, we learn who we are and the kind of person we are, from the reactions of other people to us. This learning begins at an early stage and by the end of childhood the individual would have acquired notions and feelings about self and others, about a wide array of different kinds of psychological objects. Attitudes are a result of kinds of physical and social stimulations, which a person encounters continually or repeatedly. As the boys and girls mature, their attitudes and beliefs develop and change as a result of the influence of their families. Community religion, caste and peer culture and the impact of various enculturation processes, including education, also affect attitudinal change. Results of the Purdue University polls of young people conducted by Remmers (1952) show that students become more realistic and perhaps less idealistic in their attitudes, as they grow towards maturity.

The relevant beliefs, feelings and response tendencies packed up in an individual constitute his/her attitude towards a particular object. As the individual acquires more and more stable attitudes, his improvisations, fresh examinations and interpretations decrease. His actions and reactions tend to become stereotyped, predictable and consistent.

The most important attitudes of children are those, which they develop towards the members of various groups, which make up society. These 'intergroup attitudes' determine the extent to which a child can work effectively with others on common problems or towards a common goal; they indicate the nature and outcomes of the operation of socialization processes.

The group affiliations of the individual play vital role in the formation of his attitudes. Both the members of the groups with which the individual affiliates himself and the non-membership groups to which he/she aspire to belong are important in shaping his attitudes. But the individual does not passively absorb the prevailing or dominant attitudes in the various groups to which he is affiliated. Attitudes, like cognitions, develop selectively in the process of need satisfaction. The individual will pick and choose from among the attitudes offered to him or her, those which are want-satisfying and those, which are more or less consistent with his cognitive structure and affective constellation. Every individual affiliates with many groups, which may endorse congruent or incongruent attitudes. The effect of group influences on the formation of attitudes is thus indirect and complex and seems to be determined, at least in part by the principle of 'cognitive consonance'.

Newcomb (1943) listed the conditions conducive to attitude change as (i) increased familiarity, (ii) college experience, (iii) propaganda, and (iv) mass communication. He also pointed out that attitudes would tend to be 'frozen' as individuals acquire habitual frames of reference for perceiving things. Certain frames of reference related to goals which are important to one individual become dominant over others so that, the value-systems and broad general attitudes are developed. Attitudes tend to persist when individuals continue to perceive objects with a stable frame of reference. These frames of reference may be changed by persuasion as well as by changing events. Rosenberg (1965, pp. 248) while attempting to workout a 'structural theory' of attitude dynamics concluded: A large part of the available experimental literature on attitude change may be interpreted as below:

i. the content and organization of the change – inducing communication,
ii. the individual's level of tolerance for, affective-cognitive inconsistency,
iii. the relation of the attitude to other attitudes held by the same individual,

as the important parameters associated with attitude change (abridged).

Attitudes can be changed through *persuasion*. The celebrated work of Carl Hovland, at Yale University in the 1950s and 1960s, helped to advance knowledge of persuasion. In Hovland's view, we should understand attitude change as a response to communication. He and his colleagues did experimental research into the factors that can affect the persuasiveness of a message:

1. **Target characteristics:** These are characteristics that refer to the person who receives and processes a message. One such is *intelligence* - it seems that more intelligent people are less easily persuaded by one-sided messages. Another variable that has been studied in this category is *self-esteem*. Although it is sometimes thought that those higher in self-esteem are less easily persuaded, there is some evidence that the relationship between self-esteem and persuasibility is actually curvilinear, with people of moderate self-esteem being more easily persuaded than both those of high and low self-esteem levels. The mind frame and *mood* of the target also plays a role in this process.

2. **Source characteristics:** The major source characteristics are *expertise*, *trustworthiness* and *attractiveness*. The credibility of a perceived message has been found to be a key variable here (Hovland & Weiss, 1951); if one reads a report on health and believes it comes from a professional medical journal, one may be more easily persuaded than if one believes it is from a popular newspaper. Some psychologists have debated whether this is a long-lasting effect. But Hovland and Weiss (1951) found the effect of telling people that a message came from a credible source disappeared after several weeks (it is so-called "*sleeper effect*"). This sleeper effect has become controversial. Received wisdom is that if people are informed of the source of a message before hearing it, there is less likelihood of a sleeper effect than if they are told a message and then told its source.

3. **Message characteristics:** The nature of the message plays a role in persuasion. Sometimes presenting both sides of a story is useful to help a change in attitudes.

4. **Cognitive routes:** A message can appeal to an individual's cognitive evaluation, and thus help to change an attitude. In the central route to persuasion, the individual is presented with the data and motivated

to evaluate the data and arrive at an attitude changing conclusion. In the peripheral route to attitude change, the individual is encouraged to not look at the content but at the source. This is commonly seen in modern *advertisements* that feature *celebrities*, and in some cases, *doctors* and experts.

1.2 HISTORICAL BACKGROUND OF RESEARCH ON ATTITUDE CHANGE

1.2.1 Significant phases and developments in the attitude change research

Attitude research started way back in 1918 and flourished for nearly thirty years. Asch (1948, 1952) brought a 'perceptual theory approach' to attitude change. The focus of attention shifted for some time to the field of group dynamics, but it shifted back to the area of attitudes in the 1950's. Thanks mainly to the initiative of Carl Hovland. Brisk projects were taken up at Yale by, Hovland (1957) Sherif and Hovland (1961). Chamberlin (1965) tried to explain attitude change on the basis of the method of 'strong experience'. Campbell and Lavine (1965) studied inter group relations as factors relating to attitude change. Another development in the field of attitude research started when Festinger (1957) Rosenberg (1965), Freedman (1965), Ableson et al. (1968) studied attitudes systems in the consistency theory researches and focused on the relations between attitudes on various issues, like belief and behaviour. Further, the 'Functionary Theory' work started by Smith, Bruner and White (1956) Katz and Stotland (1959). Then the mechanism underlying attitude change was studied by Kelman (1961) in his work on 'source effects' followed by Anderson (1961) on 'order effects'. In 1959, Greenwald et al. advanced the 'Response contagion Theory' of attitude change. McGuire (1968) formulated his 'Information processing' approach to attitude change. In 1971, Te Deschi et al. explained the phenomenon of attitude change through their impression management Theory and Anderson (1971) through his 'Information-integration Theory'. After that Bem (1972)· Lepper et al. (1973)· Green and Nisbett (1974) advanced their 'self-perception theory'. Then Insko et al. (1975) put forth their 'Balance Theory' of attitude change and in the same year Wyer (1974) studied the 'Attribution phenomena', while Wicklund (1974) tried to interpret attitude change by means of his 'Reactance Theory'. In 1975, Ebbesen formulated the 'Self-control Theory' of attitude change incorporating 'incentive effect'. Then David C. Perry, Kay Bussey and Judy Fischer (1980) studied the effect of rewarding children for resisting temptation on attitude change in the 'Forbidden toy paradigm'. In 1982, Jastrebske studied the role of experimenter and confederate reactions to counter-attitudinal, post-description opinion realignment in forced-compliance paradigm, following Festinger-Carlsmith's procedure.

1.3 THEORIES OF ATTITUDE FORMATION AND CHANGE

Learning theories of attitude change or, no longer as popular as they once were, focus on reinforced behavior as the primary factor responsible for attitude development. Early research on attitude change drew on Festinger's cognitive dissonance theory, which posits that, when a person is persuaded to act in a way that is not congruent with a pre-existing attitude, he or she may change the attitude to reduce dissonance (Smith & Ragan, 1999). To use dissonance to produce attitude change, the persuader must first establish the dissonance, and then provide a method to reduce it. Ideally, this will involve making the chosen alternative attractive, showing a social group with the desired attitude, demonstrating the issue's importance, providing free choice, and establishing a wide latitude of acceptance through successive approximation (Martin & Briggs, 1986).

Similarly, consistency theories assume that individuals need to have consistency between and among their attitudes and behaviors and will modify one or both to achieve this balance (Zimbardo & Leippe, 1991). Affective-cognitive consistency theory examines the relationship between attitudes and beliefs and posits that individuals are in an unstable state when their attitudes towards an object, event or person and their knowledge about that object, event, or person are inconsistent (Simonson & Maushak, 2001). This theory suggests that the affective component of the attitude system may be changed by providing new information (changing the cognitive component) via a persuasive message. Once the individual has processed the new information, he or she will undergo an attitude change to bring the knowledge and affect into harmony. Processing the message requires that the audience pay attention to and comprehend the message, then accept and retain it (Zimbardo & Leippe, 1991). Affective-cognitive consistency theory suggests that the affective component of the attitude system may be changed by first changing the cognitive component through providing new information. It does not matter how the new cognition is produced, but only that it occurs. Thus, any of the learning theories discussed in this e-book may be used in conjunction with this approach.

Social judgment theories emphasize the role of prior attitudes in shaping attitude formation and change. They describe attitude as a kind of spectrum with a "latitude of acceptance" surrounding a current attitude; a new position is more likely to be accepted if it falls within this latitude and less likely to be accepted (Smith & Ragan, 1999). This theory suggests that change in attitude position might be greater in response to the presentation of a moderate persuasive position than in response to a more extreme message.

Social learning theory focuses on the development of cognitions related to the expected outcome of behavior. This theory suggests that an individual learns attitudes by observing the behaviors of others and modeling or imitating them. An observed behavior does not have to be reinforced to be learned (Zimbardo & Leippe, 1991), and the model "can be presented on film, by television, in a novel, or by other vicarious means" (Martin & Briggs, 1986, pp. 28) The model must be credible to the target audience (Bednar & Levie, 1993). Credibility is largely a function of expertise and trustworthiness. Observational learning is greater when models are perceived as powerful and/or warm and supportive, and "imitative behavior is more likely when there are multiple models doing the same thing" (Zimbardo & Leippe, 1991, pp. 51). While "attitudes formed through direct experience with the attitude object or issue are more predictive of behavior than those formed more indirectly" (Zimbardo & Leippe, 1991, pp. 193), "media can substitute, for many live experiences" (Wetzel et al. 1994, pp. 26). Thus, observing a model via video is a viable method of learning a new attitude. For passive learners, instruction delivered by media may facilitate the rapid acquisition of complex affective behaviors more effectively than live demonstrations. However, receivers may attend mediated messages less closely than those presented directly, thereby diminishing their effectiveness (Bednar & Levie, 1993). These social learning theories of attitude change are closely related to theories that emphasize the role of social learning in cognitive development.

1.3.1. General theories of attitude change

Many theories have been formulated by different persons often on the basis of experimental evidence or with confirmation or support from such evidence, explaining attitude change in terms of factors that facilitate or cause such change, have formulated many theories. A brief review of the major theories of attitude change is attempted below:

(a) Perceptual theory: Asch (1948, 1952)

This theory relies on the fact that persuasion consists not so much changing the beliefs and opinion about a given object but rather in changing one's perception of the object.

(b) Learning theory: Hovland, Campbell & Anderson (1957)

The essence of this theory is to predict the relation-ship between a given independent variable and attitude change in terms of the hypothetical relationships of that independent variable to learning, positing that learning of the persuasive material would be conducive to attitude change.

(c) Cognitive dissonance theory: Festinger (1957)

This is one of the most influential theories of attitude change. According to it, one tends to absorb without difficult information or feelings that are in consonance with the cognitive structure already existing in him and tends to reject information and feelings that are in dissonance with it, unless the new input is so strong and convincing and persuasive as to replace the old with the new or at least to restructure it so significantly as to effect a marked change in attitude. In other words, assimilation and accordance would be easy and smooth when there is cognitive consonance between the old and the new, and cognitive dissonance between the two creates difficulty and makes for either rejection of the new, if it is weak or change cognitive structure in attitude, if it is strong, powerful and persuasive.

(d) Consistency theory: Ableson and Rosenberg (1958)

The basic notion of the consistency theory is that a person adjusts his attitudes and behaviour in such a way as to maximize internal harmony within his belief system and between his beliefs and these overt actions. He tends not toward a strictly logical consistency, but toward a more demanding 'psycho logic' containing axioms not required by strict logic.

(e) Functional theory: Katz (1960)

Katz and Stotland (1959); Katz (1960). This approach lays down the functional relationship between a person's attitude toward an object and his information about it, his perception of it, and to some extent his behaviour regarding it. Attitudes are viewed as determined by his needs in ways that might have very little to do with the particular object toward which the attitude is directed. Hence attitude change is achieved not so much by changing the person's information about, perception of, or behaviour toward the object, but rather, by changing the believer's underlying motivations and personality needs.

(f) Response contagion theory: Nuttin (1968)

In a report of thirteen experiments relating to Festinger and Carlsmith's Paradigm, Nuttin (1968) found that concluding some non-verbal-visual communication treatments along with high and low reward conditions led to a number of unexpected findings that suggested that low reward might be disturbing, non-fitting with the situation or insulting. Pursuing this idea, Nuttin found attitude change under counter-attitudinal conditions when subjects were insulted, given illegitimate examination points, or embarrassed. Nuttin proposed that these as well as dissonance treatments perturb subjects and thereby produce a state of general arousal that can cause change in evaluative responses by a non-cognitive process. If the first response, namely, advocacy act and it the second, attitude assessment, are made in close proximity during a state of arousal the second response acquires a contagion from the first response and tends to take on its pervading characteristics. Without more testing, it is difficult to assess the merit of this theory.

(g) Information-integration theory: Anderson (1976)

This theory characterizes attitude change as a two--stage process of valuation and integration. Valuation involves the assignment of a scale value and a weight to the information, with acceptance or yielding processes reflected. In the weight or importance of the information. Integration is how various items of weighted information are combined. This theory has provided a framework to research on a variety of empirical phenomena, such as resistance to persuasion induced by prior messages (Farkas and Anderson, 1976), resistance to persuasion induced by information integration (Himmelfarb, 1974), attitude change through group discussion (Anderson, 1976) etc.

(h) Impression management theory: Te deschi et al. (1971)

This theory stems from self-presentational and symbolic interaction views of social behaviour. The basic notion is that people engage in activities that develop and maintain particular identities and that through impression management people control how they are seen by others and, in turn, how they see themselves. The theory argues that, in general, people strive to maintain consistent impressions in order to enhance their credibility to others. Counter-attitudinal behaviour creates a serious management predicament because it frequently involves lying and bringing aversive consequences to others that cause the individual to appear both to him and to others socially unattractive and immoral. The individual tends to account for such behaviours through 'excuses' that make possible the denial of responsibility for actions and through 'justifications' that acknowledge responsibility but minimize the negative consequences actions.

(i) Self perception theory: Bem (1972); Lepper (1973)

According to this theory, under 'mild threat' children attribute their avoidance activity to a lack of interest, whereas under 'severe threat', subjects attribute their avoidance to threat. In the absence of extrinsic justification, the children infer that they must be avoiding the object because they want to, and devaluation follows. Severe threat leads to the inference that one is forced to behave in this way by external pressure and devaluation does not occur.

(j) Self-control theory : Ebbesen et al. (1973)

This theory claims that both severe and mild threats are sufficient to prevent the children from play with the Forbidden toy - but that the two types of threat arouse different amounts of frustration in the child. In the severe-threat condition the threat is severe enough to prevent the forbidden toy from being considered as a play object but not when the threat is mild. Children cannot escape the frustration engendered from thinking about the tempting object. Therefore one way of dealing with greater frustration in the mild threat condition is to devalue the forbidden toy.

(k) Balance theory: Insko et al. (1975)

This theory was formulated in an attempt to interpret the 'Festinger-Carlsmith Paradigm'. According to this theory, the crucial cognitive band by which the perceiver represents the situation is as follows. The self (+) is responsible for (?) arguing that the task as not enjoyable (-). If the self is positively evaluated and the counter-attitudinal act leads to negative consequences, balance depends on whether the subject accepts responsibility for the act. This theory appears to account satisfactorily for the attitudinal effects of counter attitudinal behavior, but it does not yield any new insights or make predictions that differ from those of dissonance or self-perception theories.

To conclude the eleven theories outlined above emphasize different factors and internal processes as facilitating/obstructing and effecting attitude change. They have to be seen as complementary rather than contradictory, each stressing a part of the total picture or process; some are not only similar and akin to each other, but even overlapping.

1.3.2. Trends in Indian studies on attitudes

Hundreds of studies of attitudes have been conducted in different parts of India. Many of them sought to survey the attitudes of different groups and sub-groups toward different system components and issues of topical interest. Some went further to correlate different attitudes to certain demographic or personal variables. A few experimental studies on attitude development/change have also been conducted more to assess the effects of certain techniques and programmes than to formulate or test any theory.

Sinha and Upadhyaya (1960) studied about the persistence of stereotypes in attitudes of university students toward different ethnic groups. Pareek (1968), conducted studies in measuring the attitudes of school children toward various educational system components like examinations, teachers, and different subjects of the curriculum. Ahluwalia (1978) developed scales to measure certain attitudes of teachers; Nayar (1975) also constructed and standardized the Mysore Teacher Attitude Scales (MYTAS) -four scales - which were used in some researches with teachers and student teachers. Srivatsava and Tiwari (1979); Singh A J (1979), Srivatsava N (1981); Reddy (1981); Khatoon and Verma (1982) conducted projects to inquire into the attitudes of teachers toward teaching profession, internal assessment and influences of personal factors. Vellaisamy, M (2007) effectiveness of multimedia approach in teaching science at Upper Primary level, it is concluded that there is moderate positive relationship between learning achievement and scientific attitude. Most of these studies have been of the survey and correlation types.

1.4 NATURE AND SCOPE OF THE STUDY

In the context of the above studies, the present study would focus on three attitudes, viz., those toward casteism, family planning and manual work. Keeping view the needs and possible scope for marked change in school children and try out in an experimental set-up, alternative techniques appropriate for the school setting for changing them in the desired direction. It is hoped that if they are proved to be productive, they could be employed on a wider scale and possibly woven into the curriculum as an integral part of these like the moral and spiritual education component (with clearly formulated objectives and syllabus) added to the school curriculum in Andhra Pradesh, Karnataka and some other states.

Education in schools is given largely through instruction and partly through co-curricular activities and the way things are organized, and done. Instruction is essentially a process of communication - which is an important factor in attitude development/change. Communication in schools is effected largely through the medium of language - spoken or written. The strengths and advantages of visual, audio, audio-visual media (at least as aids) and multimedia (graphics, music, animation, audio, movies, filmstrips, etc.) are also emphasized considerably and utilized to some extent. Audio-visual aids too have been accepted as a promising strategy for effective communication, especially for conveying emotionally charged ideas and messages; and it can be introduced as curricular extra curricular activity. So, it is proposed to try-out three strategies - one predominantly of verbal communication, supplemented and supported by visual aids, the second employing dramatization and multimedia strategies in different forms, and the third making an integrated of the two.

Following the latest trends in attitude rentivity of induced attitude change research Peterson et al. (1988) study of receptivity of induced attitude change after a period of three months and a 20 week study by Andrews C. Berg. R. (2005) the researcher intends to study the rentivity of the induced attitude change, in the Indian context.

1.5 TITLE OF THE STUDY

"The influence of Teaching Techniques on Changing and Retention of Certain Attitudes among Secondary School Students - An analytical Study".

1.6 OBJECTIVES OF THE STUDY

Educational objectives have been classified and defined in terms of cognitive, affective and psychomotor outcomes. While much of the large volume of knowledge acquired year after year might be forgotten soon, the affective outcomes have better prospects greater stability over time, like cognitive and psychomotor capabilities. Like values, attitudes have a prominent place among the affective outcomes; they represent two levels in a hierarchy. Development of healthy, sound attitudes is an important component of the total function of the school and of any general education programme.

It is said that today's children are tomorrow's citizens. In the present context, we see that young students often have misguided notions and feelings about social phenomena and issues. It is the duty of all concerned, especially of the educators, to set the notions and attitudes right, in order to achieve a cohesive, peaceful and productive society. Only then would happy and harmonious socializing be possible. This necessitates the development and/or changing of many socially relevant attitudes.

Certain attitudes assume special relevance and demand urgent attention in a society in a given period. Formation and change of such attitudes, becomes the concern of the society as a whole and of education, in particular. In the present Indian context, attitudes in respect of casteism, family planning, manual work, dowry system, corruption in public life, environmental pollution, village setting and rural life, etc., seem to be of special importance.

According to common observations, our society is increasingly plagued by caste considerations, by bias and prejudice, divisions and preferences, alliances and allegations based on caste, despite our avowed faith in and commitment to equality, fraternity, secularism and socialism. Similarly, our planned and concerted efforts for improving living conditions, raising the standard and quality of life, providing suitable employment opportunities to all etc., would contribute to the establishment of a truly welfare society on firm footing, are said to be offset by the 'population explosion'. Intensive and extensive population education has been suggested as a key solution. The need for earnest population control, small family norms and family planning for better life for all, hoped that if they are proved to be productive, they could be employed on a wider scale and possibly woven into the curriculum as an integral part there of like the moral and spiritual education component (with clearly formulated objectives and syllabus) added to the school curriculum in Andhra Pradesh, Karnataka and some other states in recent times.

In spite of emphasis on job oriented education, vocationalisation of education, self employment, etc., in the academic courses and specializations, university degrees and white collar jobs continue to have prestige, so the dignity of labour as advocated by Gandhiji is emphasized in theory and in profession, but manual work continues to be looked down upon by many. Thus the need for attempting to change the attitudes of students in those areas in the right direction and studying certain techniques that seem to hold promise of reasonable effect in the normal school setting and its retentivity of the induced attitude change is of latest interest.

1.7 SIGNIFICANCE OF THE STUDY

Education in schools is given largely through instruction and partly through co-curricular activities. Instruction is essentially a process of communication-which is an important factor in attitude development/ change. Communication in schools, effected largely through the medium of language-spoken or written. The strength and advantages of visual-audio and audio, visual media (at least as aids) are also emphasized considerably and utilized to some extent. Dramatization-multimedia too has been accepted as a promising strategy for effective communication, especially for conveying emotionally charged ideas and messages; and it can be introduced as a curricular or co-curricular activity. So, it is proposed to try-out three strategies - one predominantly of verbal-visual communication, supplemented and supported by verbal-visual, the second employing dramatized-multimedia in different forms and third making as integrated approach of the two.

1.8. CHAPTERISATION OF THE THESIS

The thesis consists of five chapters as shown below. The first chapter deals with the problems under the study, the importance and the need for the study. The second chapter 'Review of related literature" deals with a brief survey of the available literature on related research. The third chapter 'Design of the study' deals with the research procedure consisting of the nature of the study, tools used, sample selected, statistical techniques applied, objectives of the study, the important terms are defined and hypotheses are framed. The fourth chapter 'Analysis, Results and interpretation' deals with analysis and interpretation of the data collected. The fifth chapter 'Summary and Conclusions' deals with the overall view of the study, major findings, concluding observations and suggestions for further research.

CHAPTER 2

REVIEW OF RELATED LITERATURE

2.1 INTRODUCTION

This chapter is meant for presenting the review of related literature and research done in the field. The broad areas in which review would be attempted are attitude scale-development and validation, attitude survey, attitude development and attitude change.

2.2 ATTITUDE SURVEY

2.2.1 General social attitudes

Only a limited number of recent studies of some substance conducted abroad and in India are reviewed under each category below.

In India, Anant (1968) attempted a similar study on adult groups in Agra, Delhi and Varanasi regions of Uttar Pradesh. The results of the two studies showed clearly that the resentment against the caste system was very much higher in South than in the North, and that there was a significant effect of education on the attitude towards casteism. The whole group responses of Anant's study were more in favour of caste system than the graduate group responses. The responses of college students were more radical than the graduate group responses while the whole group responses were the least radical.

Tuna and Livson (1960) in their study – "family, SES and adolescent attitude toward society"- tried to find the attitude toward authority, ranging from conformity to rebelliousness among 14-16 years boys and girls. They found that, in general, girls conform more than boys, further girls showed consistent increase of degree of conformity from 14 to 16 years - except that there was a decline in conformity at the age of 16. A negative relationship was found between boys' conformity and SES ratings where as significant positive relationship was found between conformity and SES ratings of girls.

Mullis and Bornhoeft (1982) studied "children's attitudes to television advertisements" and concluded that children's and adult's attitude toward TV advertisements differ and that children view TV advertisements entirely in terms of their entertainment value.

Dominique Brossard, Bruce Lowenstein, et al. (2005) conducted a study entitled "Scientific knowledge and attitude change." The results suggest that projects must make explicit to participants the issues that they are experiencing. In addition, the results suggest that more sensitive measures need to be designed to assess attitude change among environmentally aware citizens.

2.2.2 Student attitudes

Stone and Barker (1950) studied the interests and attitudes of girls (junior high schools of Berkeley, California) and concluded that more post-menocheal than pre-monocheal girls of the same chronological age showed an interest in and favorable attitude toward opposite sex.

Payne (1955) probed into the attitude of high school students and found that the boys from rural areas were significantly less favorable to the ideas of their wives working' after marriage than were boys from urban areas.

In the 1956 study conducted by Michigan Institute for Social Research involving 11-18 year girls (N=2000), it was found that they were favourably inclined toward having steady employment, interesting work and nice people to work with.

Haire and Morrison (1957) tried to find the attitude of high school children of low SES toward the problem of labour-management relations. The low-SES group tended to be strongly pro-labour.

2.3 ATTITUDE DEVELOPMENT

Attitudes of an individual are developed in the process of the satisfaction of his wants and by the information to which the individual is exposed.

2.3.1 Longitudinal studies

Longitudinal studies of child-development suggest that, as individuals mature, there are systematic 'shifts' in their mean levels of dominance, aggressiveness, competitive-ness, conformity, independence and their attitudinal tendencies. Kagan and Moss (1962), showed that attitudes towards peers rather than parents or other authority figures show systematic age trends. Bloom (1964) and Kelly (1955) found that attitude orientations, from age to age reveal fairly high test-retest-correlations. Greenstein (1965) and Hess (1965) showed systematic age trends in political attitudes from early childhood to old age.

Prawat, Rechard S et al. (1979) conducted a "Longitudinal study of attitude development in pre, early and later adolescent samples" changing in attitude were examined over a one year period in pre, early and later adolescent samples. Self-esteem, locus of control, and achievement motivation were examined. The amount of attitudinal change evidence by subjected at each age level varied with the kind of attitude bring assessed.

Croucher et al. (1982) in their study 'Pupil attitude changes to junior school activity' hypothesized that attitudes among 9-11 year old children would differ significantly between age groups and sexes such that girls and younger children world express more favorable attitudes to school activities and that attitudes would deteriorate over the school year. Initially boys showed more favorable attitude than girls toward arts and crafts, while girls had superior attitudes toward art, music and crafts. Over the next year, boys' attitudes deteriorated toward art, music and craft, while girls' attitude deteriorated toward physical education, reading and music. Attitudes are more affected by factors such as school, teaching methods and attendance than by individual differences.

Etaugh (1982) on the basis of their longitudinal study on college students found that more liberal attitudes toward women were formed with increasing years of college attendance.

In India, Shankar (1982) attempted to predict changes in social attitudes produced by community development pro-grammes. A control group with no community project programme and experimental groups with 3,7,10 and 24 years of development work were administered social distance scale at different intervals for several years. Subjects were 429 males of ten social castes. Using the number of years of project work as a predictor variable and social distance scores as the criterion variables predictions were made for the 24 year group by linear and curvilinear models. Although the curvilinear model showed the best mathematical fit, the linear medal yielded more accurate prediction than curvilinear model when compared with the scores for the 24 year group.

Alison Kelly (1986) conducted a study entitled "The development of girls' and boys' attitudes to science: A longitudinal study". Attitude-to-science tests were completed by 1300 pupils, at ten schools, when they were 11 years old and again two and a half years later. During that time their interest in most branches of science decreased, but both girls and boys became more interested in learning about human biology. Their opinions about science and scientists also became generally less favourable, but pupils grew more willing to see science as suitable for girls. There was considerable stability in the attitudes of individual children over the period of the study.

Mc Kinnon, David H et al. (2000) conducted a study entitled "Longitudinal study of student attitudes toward computers: Resolving an attitude decay paradox". Attitudes toward computer use during junior high school, where attitudes became less positive.

Anders, C. and Berg, R. (2005) conducted a study entitled on "Factors related to observed attitude change toward learning chemistry among university students". This study was completed during a 20-week, full-time introductory university chemistry course. A positive attitude change was associated with evidence of motivated behaviour, while a negative change was linked to less motivated behaviour. Students addressed similar factors in the educational setting, but students with positive attitude changes exhibited fewer negative views of educational factors while students with negative attitude changes showed an opposite pattern.

Crouter et al. (2007) studied the development of gender attitude traditionality across middle childhood and adolescence and concluded that no one longitudinal pattern captured the development of gender attitudes trajectories varied as a function of contextual and personal characteristics.

2.4 CHANGING ATTITUDES - INFLUENCING FACTORS

To structure the vast literature on attitude change in this category, Lindzey and Aronson's (1969) classification, namely (i) source factors, (ii) message factors (iii) channel factors, (iv) receiver factors, and (v) destination factors is followed. In addition to these general studies, studies which are very relevant to the present study but do not directly come under the above heads are also included.

2.4.1 Source factors

(i) Credibility and attitude change

Hovland and Weiss (1951); Hovland and Manbdell (1952), Hovland. Janis and Kelly (1953); Mausner and Mausner (1955); Aronson and Golden (1962); Watts and Mc Guire (1964); Bauer (1965) and Anderson (1965) conducted studies on the role credibility of the communicator in producing attitude change. Mc Killip (1975) studied the influence of credibility on impression formation and reported positive correlation between the two, but two other studies by Mc Peek and Edwards (1975); Mc Peek and Gross (1975) did not find so. Studies on variety of communicator behaviours that affect credibility were reported by Miller et al. (1976) - speed of speaking, London (1973) - verbal and non-verbal expression, and listen ability and vocabulary diversity.

(ii) Attractiveness of the communicator

This is determined by the receiver's similarity to or familiarity for liking for him. Sherif and Sherif (1964) observed that to produce attitude change the attractive source need not produce any evidence for the validity of his position but need only make the role relationship salient.

Newcomb (1961), Sampson and Insko (1964) have shown that ideological similarity induces familiarity and interpersonal liking and, that reverse sequence also occurs. This was confirmed by Zägnoc (1960).

A long series of studies by Stotland and Dunn (1962), has shown that Ss empathize with and adopt the feelings of others to the extent that these others have been represented similar to themselves though they find the tendency stronger in men than in women. Stotland and Patchen's (1961) results agreed with the above finding.

Byrne (1961), Byrne and Nelson (1964), Byrne and Griffitt (1966) have shown that liking of the others increases rectilinearly with the number of common attitudes that the subject is told he shares with the others.

Dymkowski (1980) in his study 'Self concept and attractiveness of source of personal information' discusses the controversies between 'self-consistency' and 'self-esteem' theories. The theories led to contradictory predictions concerning the formation and change in the attractiveness of the source. Self- consistency theory predicts that people with low-esteem will Judge the source of positive personal evaluation as less attractive than that of negative personal evaluation, while the self-esteem theory predicts the reverse.

French and Snyder (1959), Griffin and Ehrlich (1963), Horowitz et al. (1951), Sherwood (1965), Thrasher (1954), Wallach, Kogan and Bem (1962) conducted studies which show that the more the subject liked the source of a persuasive message, the more he would change his beliefs toward the position of the source.

The studies of Zimbardo (1960), Brehm and Cohen (1962) proved that under certain specified conditions, like when the receiver commit himself voluntarily to listen to a persuasive communication represented as coming from either an admirable source or a distasteful source, the source produces more opinion change - as the receiver's dislike for him increases.

Smith (1961) concluded that, if the person complies with the source's demand to engage in some counter – attitudinal behaviour, he shows more internalized opinion change, if the source with whom he complied is disliked rather than liked. This received support from the study of Zimbardo et al. (1965).

Studies of Gewritz and Baer (1958), Shallenberger and Zigler (1958) and Stevenson et al. (1963) revealed that social reinforcement influences childrens' behaviour more, if it comes from a stranger, than if it comes from a familiar person or a parent. Harvey's (1962) finding also supported this hypothesis.

Fishbein (1963), Kelly (1955) and Merton (1957) noticed that liking for the group or its members, and being liked by them - all enhance the group valence for changing the person's option to wards the group norms.

(iii) Mild vs Severe threat and attitude change

Aronson et al. (1966) found that mild threats are, under some - conditions, more effective than severe threats in changing attitudes and thus inducing long-range internalized obedience. This confirmed the earlier finding of Janis and Feshbac (1953).

The studies of Berkowitz, and Cottingham (1960), Haefner (1956), Snider (1962), Miller and Hewgill (1964, 1966), Laventhal et al. (1956), Laventhal and Niles (1964, 1965), Laventhal and Watts (1966), Laventhal, Watts and Pagano (1967), dealt with a wide variety of issues - including smoking-cancer relationship, dental cares, tetanus, serious injury in auto-accident due to failure of seatbelts, employing a wide variety of subjects and a number of orthogonal independent variables. They found 'positive relationship between intensity of fear-arousal and amount of attitude change, whereas it is not equally applicable to all possible cases and to all dependent variables covered in the studies.

Beach (1966), and Robbins (1962) found no relationship between the two variables mentioned above.

Insko (1965) found that high fear arousal is more effective in convincing non-smokers that they should not develop the habit but there is no difference between the high and low fear messages in inducing belief change about deleterious effects of smoking upon health.

(iv) Power and attitude change

Festinger and Thibaut (1951) and Gerard (1953) have shown that when the group members exert more influence over one another, the task allows more deviation.

In 1951, Alberta and Siegel of Stanford University tested the assumption that both the reference and membership groups of a person affect his attitudes. Their sample consisted of three experimental groups of college fresh women. Their conclusion was that the attitudes of the girls were determined by the groups they wanted to belong to and by the combined influence of these two kinds of groups. Burdick (1955), Dittes and Kelly (1956), Kelman (1958), Mc Bride (1954), Raven and French (1958) found that where the person is complying with a power of source, the person will be more influenced regards his public responses (which the source can detect) than as regards his more private opinions. In other words, the real change is not in the internalized attitude, but in the studied behavior of the subject.

(v) Source valence and attitude change

Hovland, Janis and Kelly (1953), Bauer (1965) found that a message was perceived and evaluated, depending on whether its purported source was positively or negatively valanced.

Hovland and Wiss (1951), Hovland and Mandell (1952) found that there was no difference in recall due to source valence, though Mc Guire (1957) presented results, which suggested that learning plays a significant role in mediating the source-persuasion relationship.

Kelman and Hovland (1953), Bauer (1965) found that when the purported source is clearly positively valanced or subject negatively, valanced, the subject/used the information as a cue to accept or reject the conclusion of the message without really absorbing the arguments used.

2.4.2. Message factors

Most research in the area of attitudes centred on the message factors which could be classified as: (1) types of persuasive appeals, (2) inclusions and omissions from the message, (3) order of presentation within the message and (4) source-receiver discrepancy.

(1) Types of persuasive appeals

(i) Self-insight and attitude change

Stotland, Katz and Patchen (1959) in their work tried to change the attitudes by presenting to the believer, case history material, which demonstrates a person holding an ethnic prejudice similar to his own psychodynamic reasons that are less than admirable. But the results were not very encouraging.

Shrauger (1975) in his study 'Responses to evaluation as a function of initial self-perceptions' tried to determine the effect of discrepancies between initial attitudes towards one-self and evaluative feed back and concluded that the differences are not significant and that further probe is required.

(ii) Humour and attitude change

Lull (1940) found that the addition of humour to a speech on a serious topic, affected neither its persuasiveness nor its interestingness as judged.

Windies (1961) concluded that receiver's persuasive-ness could be enhanced, by putting him in a pleasant mood while receiving the message, even when the mood is achieved such issue irrelevant inductions as a humorous introduction.

Gruner (1965) found that satirical speeches were significantly no persuasive. But practised satire is often used as an instrument of attempted attitude change.

(iii) Logical vs emotional appeals and attitude change

Chen (1935), Knower (1935), Matnews (1947) and Weiss (1960) concluded on the basis of their studies that there is no difference in the effectiveness of logical and emotional appeals. Manefee and Granneberg (1940), and Eldersveld (1956) found that emotional appeals have more impact than logical appeals.

Biggers and Bert (1982) conducted an experiment with 60 high school students using a 2×3 design to explore the relationship between feelings of pleasure and arousal elicited by an environment and ratings of source credibility, and attitude change. Three levels of pleasure and two levels of arousal were combined factorially. Results suggested that the emotion eliciting qualities of the experimenter could be used to predict both source credibility and attitude change.

(iv) Reinforcement and attitude change

Reinforcement can take several forms. The most common form that was first used by Ekman (1958), Hildum and Brown (1956) and Insko (1965), is an approbation by the experimenter when the subject expresses the opinion desired to be learned. They concluded that this type of social reinforcement is generally as successful in manipulating attitude as it is in manipulating other forms of behavior.

Janis, Kaye and Kirschner (1965) indoctrinated persons by engaging them in a pleasant or unpleasant activity while hearing desired or undesired political slogans. They found that students show more opinion change if they received reinforcement through a snack.

Weiss (1960), Weiss, Rawson and Pasamanick (1963) used reinforcement in the persuasive communication as a part of the message itself. They showed that the strength of an opinion can be enhanced by the immediacy with which arguments are presented after that opinion is expressed.

(v) Style of the message and attitude change

Taylor (1952) found that propagandizing skill of speeches as rated by speech experts had very little relationship to their persuasive effectiveness, while Bettinghaus (1961) found that delivery effectiveness as rated by judges did predict significantly the attitude-change impact of the speeches.

Dietrich (1946) found that dynamic presentation was less-effective in producing attitude change when compared to a subdued-presentation. Bowers (1964) found that speeches involving more- intense words, qualified nouns and metaphors produced lower attitude change in some cases and no difference in others. Carmichael and Cronkhite (1965) used the same material as Bowers, but found a slight, non-significant tendency for the more intense speeches to produce less attitude change, whereas Boradac and Osborn (1966) varied high intensity versus low intensity by use of metaphorical versus literal conclusions to speeches and found that metaphorical presentation produced significantly greater attitude change.

(vi) Implicit vs explicit conclusion and attitude change

Hovland and Mandell (1952) in their study, used the explicit - conclusion form ending with a statement of the conclusion while their implicit-conclusion form left out of the final statement. The result was a highly significant difference in favour of the explicit- conclusion form.

This was supported by the studies of Cooper and Dinerman (1951), Hadley (1953), Mc Keachie (1954), Fine (1957) and Maier and Maier (1957).

Cohen (1959), Mc Guire (1960), Stotland, Ksatz and Patchen (1959) showed that more time is required for the implicit-conclusion message to be grasped by the unorganized, unintelligent or unmotivated subject, whereas Cooper and Dinerman (1951) found the greater effectiveness for explicit over implicit conclusion to be more pronounced in subjects of lesser intelligence than in more intelligent subjects. Hovland and Mandell's (1952) studies did not find it so. Katz (1959) study revealed that the more subtle implicit conclusion communication is more effective with people who are only moderate rather than high in ego defensiveness. The study of Mc Guire (1960) indicated that the actual opinion change is less than that predicted while the studies of Dillehay, Insko and Smith (1966), Evans, Rozelle, Noblit and Williams (1975) did not find it so.

(vii) Refuting Vs ignoring of opposition arguments and attitude change

A study of Hovland et al. (1959) revealed that refuting the opposition was more effective with those of high intelligence and ignoring it with those of low intelligence. Subsequent studies by Janis, Lumbsdaine and Gladstone (1951) and of Paulson (1954) indicated that refuting and ignoring the opposition arguments were about equally effective, over all, in producing attitude change. But Lumsdaine and Janis's (1952) study indicated that refuting the opposition arguments rather than ignoring them was much more effective in producing subsequent resistance to counter attacks.

Annis and Meier (1934), Asch (1956), Cromwell and Kuchel (1952), Dietsoh and Gurnee (1948) and Stukat (1958) confirmed that certain amount of repetition does facilitate attitude change but the asymptote is quickly reached.

2. Structure of presentation and attitude change

(i) Ordering with respect to desirability and agreeability and agreeability and attitude change

A communication situation in which a source has to address himself to various topics and during which he will have to argue for agreeable position on some issues and disagreeable ones on the others, raises the question of optimal ordering of topics for producing maximum opinion change cross all the issues. Mc Guire (1957) argued, on the basis of learning theory, that the agreeable position – first-strategy would be more effective, since the agreeable news in the early part of the message would reinforce and motivate the subject to listen to the subsequent points of the message. In his study Mc Guire (1957) found that agreeable-disagreeable order produced significantly more opinion change and that learning of the message content tends to confirm his hypotheses about the mediatory role of learning.

Weiss (1957) supported the above finding and concluded that the effect stems from the source's acquisition of positive valence through his association with the earlier agreeable messages.

(ii) Climax vs anticlimax and attitude change

Mc Guire (1957) suggested that one should capitalize on attention when one has it and present strong arguments first.

Weiss (1963) contended that arguments are reinforces and that strong arguments yield larger rewards and so climax order is more effective than the anti-climax and Andereon's (1959) work lent support to this order.

(iii) Primacy v recency effects and attitude change

Hovland and Mandell (1952), Hovland, Campbell and Brock (1957), Miller and Campbell (1959) 'were of the opinion that the effect of primacy and regency in opinion change could be explained in terms of the underlying learning process. As regards to initial learning, the primacy effect is favoured because pro-active inhibition is operative, to that learning of the first-side tends to interfere with learning the opposite second side. On the other hand retention favours the second side since it is close to the final phase of opinion change. Insko (1964) confirmed the above hypothesis in his study.

Anderson and Barrios, A.A. (1961) and Anderson (1965) supported the pro-active inhibition model though Anderson does not regard the memory interpretation as adequate.

The perceptual theory of 'order effects' tends to predict 'Primary effects'. This was formulated by Sherif (1935) and supported by Asch (1952). It contends that one's early familiarization with a situation establishes a frame of reference set, towards which all subsequent experience is assimilated and interpreted. Sherif's (1935) experiment demonstrated that sets seem to be formed very rapidly in the early stages of acquaintance. Hence primacy effects become less pronounced as the messages deal with material familiar to the receiver.

Anderson and Barrios (1961) found that primacy effect declines with practice at an impression formation task. An interaction effect in the opposite direction was first reported by Lana (1961, 1963), while they found no interaction in either direction in later experiments.

Taking it for granted that conclusions are drawn explicitly, Mc Guire (1964) conducted studies on 'order 'efforts' - conclusion first or last. It deals with the primacy-regency question in attitude change and personality impression formation. He suggested that each position has its own advantages and can be equally effective in producing attitude change.

(iv) Unexpected communication and attitude change

Eagly and Chaiken (1975, 1976)· Mc Killip (1975), Mc Killip and Edwards (1975) found that unexpected communications are especially persuasive, whereas two other studies by Mc Peek and Edwards (1975) Mc Peek and Gross (1975) did not find it so.

Wood, Eagly and Chaiken (1977) found that a message is more persuasive and the communicator rated as more unbiased when the advocated position was unexpected in terms of either type of inferred basis.

(v) Repetition of the persuasive message and attitude change

Hull's (1933) work applying learning concepts to hypnosis and suggestibility shed some light on the effect of repetition on persuasion. Peterson and Thrustone (1933) found that several commercial films seemed to produce a sizable attitude change effect even when no one film was found to produce significant impact. Staats and Staats (1958) found that in very sample verbal conditioning situations, compliance increases with repetition. Asch (1956) and Stukat (1958) showed that in conformity situations, the impact increases as the size of the unanimous majority grows from one to four persons.

3. Discrepancy and attitude change

Ostrom, Stelle and Smilansky (1974) and Nemeth and Endicott (1976) found that at least up to extreme discrepancies, the amount of attitude change obtained is a negatively accelerated increasing function of the discrepancy between the receiver's and message's positions. In their studies, the message consisted in an argumentative communication.

Fisher, Rubinstein and Freeman (1956), Goldberg (1954), and Zimbardo (1960) in their studies used a message which was simply a normative feedback of the author's position and confirmed the above result.

But Brehm and Lispher (1959) suggested that the positive relationship is clearer if the message does not contain arguments for its position but is simply a source endorsement.

Sherif and Hovland (1961) formulated the assimilation contrast theory which states that maximal attitude change is produced when the message takes a position that is of moderate discrepancy from the recipients own initial disposition--specifically when it falls in the zone of indifference.

2.4.3. Channel factors

(i) *Medium of communication and attitude change*

Mc Luhan (1964) and Mc Luhan and Fiore (1967) conducted studies on 'verbal happenings' and concluded that the medium through which the message is communicated has more impact on the receiver than does the message content. Eiser and Mowerwhite (1969) demonstrated that individual's attitudes are changed in accordance with evaluative verbal labels that are used to conceptualize the attitude continuum.

Allport (1935), and Knower (1935, 1936) tried to find out whether the written or the spoken word has more persuasive impact. None of them found any significant difference between the two modalities.

Harwood (1951), Beighley (1952), Haugh (1952), Young (1953), Stromer (1954) and Toussaint (1960) concluded on the basis of their studies that comprehension is greater with read than hearing. Since comprehension would, every thing else being equal, be positively related to persuasive impact, there must be greater yielding in the reading than in the bearing situation.

Wittaker and Meade (1967) reported that male sources are perceived as more credible with oral than with written messages. Agreed with this finding and concluded that this was due to the fact that the subject might feel greater anxiety or greater pressure from self- interest or good taste, to conform when the more personalized spoken modality is used. (He controlled this physical presence of the source, using face-to-face and taped oral presentation).

Rosenthal's (1967) work on para-linguistic communication and experimenter effects, has demonstrated sex-related differences between sight and sound as modes of communicating unintended social influence. His experimenter-bias research, studied non-verbal clues of both auditory and visual nature used by experimenters, consciously or unconsciously, to shape the behaviour of the subjects. His work suggests that non-verbal communication a very complex, worked with elaborate pictorial material as non-verbal communication while Mc Luhan (1964) used non-verbal communication via the mediator himself, and found them effective.

Rowley and Keller (1962) concluded that the operant -conditioning theory supports the superiority of verbal over visual clues in shaping human behaviour.

(ii) Mass media effectiveness on attitude change

The studies of Berelson, Lazarsfeld and Mc Phee (1954), Hovland and Janis (1959), Belson (1961) and Kraus (1962) found that attitude change is much lees in a gross-behaviour situation such as bullying or voting.

Berelson, Lazarsfeld and Mc Phee (1954) found that those who expose themselves most to the presidential campaigns on the mass media seem to be the least affected by the campaign.

Kraus (1962) in his studies on the Presidential Elections in the U.S. showed that face-to-face informal communication among peers is much more effective than exposure to mass- media in affecting voting behaviour.

Bradac, Konsky and Davies (1976), Williams (1975) concluded that live or videotaped messages induce greater opinion change than audio-taped messages, which in turn, elicit greater change than written messages. But Silverthrone at al (1975) Worchel et al. (1975), had inconsistent findings on this. Eagly and Chaiken (1975) found that the written modality is superior in conveying information-especially material which is difficult to understand.

(iii) Distraction and attitude change

Insko, Turn- bull and Yandell (1974) distinction between distractions involving orientation primarily to the communication (message set) or to the distracting task (task set). They found that the message set produced a decrease in counter - argumentation resulting in increased attitude change while the task set involved devaluation of the communication and decrement in recall - resulting in a decrease in attitude change.

(iv) Group discussion Vs lecture and attitude change

The effect of group decision upon the action and attitudes of individuals. Their objective was to change strongly held, traditional good preference through interesting lecture versus group discussion and decision.

A study Bennett (1955) attempted to disentangle the relative contributions of lecture versus discussion, decision versus discussion, degree of commitment to adopt a recommended practice, the degree of actual or perceived consensus in the group. He concluded that group discussion and public commitment were not more effective than the lecture method and private commitment respectively. But, this was questioned by a study of Pennington, Hararey and Base (1958). They found that opinion change was greater when discussion was allowed than when no discussion took Place. Discussion may be more effective than the lecture method when a consensus is sought, but no more effective when the members of a group are asked to make individual decisions.

2.4.4 Receiver factors

(i) Active participation and attitude change

Learning theories have emphasized active recitation/participation as enhancing learning or internalization. This was confirmed by the results obtained by Janis and King (1954), King and Janis (1956) did suggest that calling on the subject to improvise a speech produced more attitude change than having him read silently or aloud, a prepared speech. But the results obtained by Zimbardo et al. (1965) did not reach the conventional level of significance. The study of Stanley and Klausmier (1957) also failed to confirm the above pre-diction, whereas Greenbaum (1963), Jansen and Stolurow (1962), Mc Guire (1961), Mc Guire and Papageorgis (1961), came up with significant results in the opposite direction showing that more opinion change occurred with passive reading than with active improvisation.

Mc Guire (1964), and Mc Guire and Papageorgis (1961) produced evidence that the opportunity for active participation does tend to catch up with passive reading in effective-ness, provided that an extrinsic threat is added to motivate the believer or sufficient time is allowed for the receiver to develop supportive material.

Petty, Cacioppo and Rachel (1981) on the basis of their study on personal involvement and persuasion on 145 undergraduates, found that an increase in involvement is associated with an increase in acceptance of the message argument because people are motivated to hold correct and defensible opinions and they have a better frame work for things that are relevant to the self.

(ii) Role playing and attitude change

In a laboratory study of the influence of role playing upon attitudes toward the Culbertson (1957) administered pre-experimental attitude scales to a sample of subjects to measure the valence of their attitudes toward Negro-white housing integration and of their generalized attitudes toward Negroes. She then divided her subjects into group of six, each group consisting of three role players and three observers. Each observer was instructed to watch a particular role player. Her results indicate that a significantly larger percentage of role players than observers became more positive toward integration. Also a higher percentage of observers shifted than did control subjects who had not attended any role playing session.

Janis and King (1954, pp. 260) of Yale communication and attitude change programme studied the effect of role playing upon change in beliefs of their student subjects. They concluded that a persons belief's would be changed if he is stimulated to think of new arguments and appeals in order to convince others to adopt a point of view and that 'satisfaction' with performance in role playing provides a special reward that reinforces the beliefs in playing the role. Later in their 1956 study, they investigated into the above conclusions, in their experiments on male college students, they found that there is a lowering of psychological resistance whenever a person regards the persuasive argu-ments emanating from others as his "own" ideas.

Scott (1957, 1959) in his studies investigated the effects of rewarding the verbal expression of attitude upon attitude change. His subjects were pairs of students from different psychology classes and they were made to debate one of the three different issues towards which they had earlier expressed their attitudes. Both members were required to argue for the position 'contrary' to the one they preferred. The winner of the debate was determined by the vote of the class. However, the experimenter actually manipulated the class vote so that a predetermine member of each pair won. Later on attitude tests were administered. Results showed that the 'winners' changed in the direction of the position, which they defended in the debate, while the 'losers' did not change significantly as compared to the control group. Thus he concluded that role-playing would induce attitude change only if the individual received reward for publicity espousing a view at variance with his private attitudes.

(iii) Predispositions of message recipient and attitude change

Himmelfarb and Arazi (1974) obtained a dissonance predicted interaction between choice and source attractiveness but only when a persuasive message, was very discrepant from the subject's initial opinions. Worchel and Arnold (1977) found greater change toward a message among subjects who had chosen to believe it.

The study of Worchel, Arnold and Baker (1975) suggests that recipients increase their desire to hear and are more persuaded by attitudinally discrepant messages that have been removed from hearing - unless the censor is both highly attractive and expressive. Hess (1965), Hass and Grady (1975), Cialdini (1976, Petty (1976) found that 'attitude shifts' occur subsequent to warnings, but prior to the receipt of the message.

Eagly and Warren (1976) found that intelligence showed a very slightly positive relationship to opinion change towards messages supported by complex arguments, but a stronger negative relationship to unsupported messages.

Infante (1975) found that recipients scoring high on a Richness of Fantasy Scale that estimates receiver's pre-disposition to imagine implications of a message content, showed greater opinion change than those scoring low.

(iv) Compliance and attitude change

Festinger and Carlsmith (1959) reported that subjects induced to lie for a $ 20 payment ended up in believing the lie less than a group of subjects who told the same lie for a $ 1 payment. Brehm and Cohen (1962), Lependorf (1964) showed that this effect extended down to even smaller incentives, and concluded that the less monetary incentive a person was given for his lie, the more did he believe it.

Smith (1961) Zimbardo et al. (1965) found that when military personnel were induced to eat a disliked food of fried grass-hoppers, by pleasant and unpleasant sources, more favourable attitude change toward the food occurred when the subjects complied at the behest of an unpleasant person.

Brehm and Cohen (1962) asked the Yale students to write essays favorable on the behaviour of police, at which the students were angered. The students were offered $ 0.50, $ 1, $ 2 or $ 5 to write the essays. The subjects who wrote most favorably were those who received $ 0.50 while others showed little change in favourableness. This result confirmed the dissonance theory. However, Rosenberg (1965) felt that the above experiment was inadequate and took great pairs in repeating the experiment in which conditions for reward were isolated from the situation where beliefs were measured. He concluded that, as the amount of reward increases, there is a direct linear increase in agreement with the antifeeling and the greater the reward, the greater is the attitude change.

Freedman (1963) found that when subjects agreed to perform, a dull task, they showed greater liking for the task, if, prior to their performance, they were told that the study was of low, than high value to the experimenter.

In the classic studies conducted by Asch (1951,1956), he found that 32% of his subjects were able to maintain relative independence of their beliefs in a social pressure situation inducing attitude change.

Allen and Levin (1971) in their study found out that when a majority group gave a wrong answer, the 'planted deviant' gave an answer, which was still more incorrect, but this had a powerful effect on the subject.

Milgram (1963, 1964) in his studies on compliance using a mock-electric shook on a 'learner' who was a con-federate of the experimenter, found that the subjects obeyed the experimenter even though they thought that they were hunting another person.

Bierbrauer (1973) repeated Milgram's study with tape recorded protests of the learner and the subjects showed lower, compliance rates than were actually obtained by Milgram.

Aronson and Carlsmith (1963) and Freedman (1965) found that if a child obeys a mild request - 'not to play with an attractive toy' - he will come to believe that the toy is not as attractive as he first thought. If, instead of a mild request, a strong command with threat of punishment for playing with the toy is given the child tends to assume that he likes the toy.

Gerard, Conolley and Wilhemy (1974) proposed a U-shaped relationship between attitude change and the 'resultant justification'. They claim that when the resultant justification is insufficient, dissonance will be aroused and reduced by changing one's attitude to bring it in line with the commitment. As it increases to a zone of sufficiency dissonance and attitude change would decrease. As the resultant justification passes beyond the sufficiency zone and becomes overly sufficient, attitude change increases by an Incentive or secondary reinforcement- type process.

Perry, Kay and Fischer (1980) studied the effects of rewarding children for resisting temptation on attitude change in the forbidden-toy paradigm. They tested the hypo-thesis that promising children an extrinsic reward for not deviating would prevent them from deviating from an activity under mild threat because it would provide an alternative external locus to which they could attribute their avoidance. They conducted two experiments. Results of I experiment with 54, 6-7 year old supported the hypothesis. However, in experiment II with 72, 6 year olds, it was shown that giving subjects an expectation of reward that was not contingent on avoiding the forbidden activity also pre-vented devaluation under mild threat. These results disconfirmed the predictions of the 'self-control' theory. Here, reward expectancy is considered to distract mild threat subjects from experiencing the frustration that causes them to devalue the activity as well as to detract severe threat subjects from concentrating on the pleasurable aspects of the activity, which ordinarily prevents devaluation under severe threat.

(v) Self attribution process and attitude change

Bem in his (1972) works tried to provide an alter-native explanation for dissonance phenomena. He argued that when internal cues are minimal or uninterpretable people infer their attitudes and other internal states primarily from their behaviour, in a manner functionally equivalent to that of external observers who must rely on external cues. Therefore, the less the behaviour appears to be under the control of the situational stimuli such as reward or justification, the greater the influence of the internal state or attitude on behavior.

Bem and Mc Connell (1970) found that initial attitudes that subjects recalled after counter attitudinal behaviour were nearly identical to their most-manipulation-attitudes. However, the studies of Aderman and Brehm (1976) found that error in recall of initial attitudes was leas when subjects were offered an incentive to recall their initial attitudes, and that the magnitude of error in, recalled initial attitude was less than half the magnitude of actual change as shown by Shaffer (1975). Studies by Ross, Shulman (1973) confirmed the dissonance theory prediction that increasing the salience of initial attitudes increases attitude change because -the counter-attitudinal behaviour becomes more dissonant, while self-perception theory would predict that salience decreases change because it increases the clarity of internal cues and thereby decreases reliance on external cues. The researches of Green (1974) and Shaffer (1974) also obtained results favoring the dissonance theory.

Kiesler and Pallak (1976) concluded that manipula-tions typically used in dissonance experiments cause a state of arousal. Zanna, Higgins and Taves (1976) reported findings on the misattribution of arousal states produced by dissonance manipulation.

Klsler's (1971) work and the studies of Fazio, Zanna and Fazio (1980) confirm that pro-attitudinal behaviour can produce shifts in attitudes and suggest a self-inference process; yet consistent behaviour does not always produce attitude change as observed by Kiesler, Roth and Pallak (1974) and the conditions under which such shifts occur need considerable specification

The works of Hendrick and Giesen (1976) and Taylor (1975) on emotions and attitudes) suggest that subjects are aware of the disparity between the feedback and their internal feelings and try to accommodate this discrepancy.

(vi) Attribution and attitude change

Anderson (1976) in their work on 'attitude change in attribution' applied integration theory to cognitive responses and attitudes. Ross, Bierbraher and Hoffman (1976 investigated into the role of attribution processes in conformity and dissent. Other works in this field are Calder (1974) (Informational cues and attributions based on role behaviour), Miller (1966) (constraint and target effects in the attribution of attitudes), Miller et al. (1976) - attribution versus persuasion as a means of modifying behaviour. Munson and Kiesler (1974) - the role of attributions by others in the acceptance of persuasive communications. It was found in these studies that individual's attitudes and behaviour were changed merely by attributing certain attitudes or dispositional characteristics to them as well as by repeated use of behavioral measurements.

Lepper et al. (1973) could find evidence to snow that the dispositional. Attributions, once made, are difficult to reverse. In their study, a variation of the forbidden to study some children were told that all children obey and they refrain from playing with the for-bidden toy, when this was done before they entered the toy room - it destroyed the attitude change effects These children did not decrease their liking for the toy, but the dispositional attribution "I don't like the toy" made while they were in the toy room, and the knowledge that all other children would obey - did not reverse the attribution as it logically should have.

This irreversibility of dispositional attributions was demonstrated more strongly in a series of studies made by Ross et al. (1976) on high school and college students, who were led to believe that they had done either quite well or quite poorly on a novel problem- solving task. They were then debriefed. But, when the subjects were interviewed later on, it was found that the debriefing had tailed to destroy the initial attributions.

(vii) Age, intelligence and attitude change

Barber and Calverley (1964), Messerschmidt (1933) concluded on the basis of their experiments that maximum attitude change is generally found at about 8 or 9 years of age.

Hull (1933), and Stukat (1958) found that after a chronological age of about 9 years, there is a clear decline in suggestibility until the end of adolescence, after which it levels off.

Hovland and Janis (1959) concluded studies which showed that persuasiblity declines with age more for boys than for girls.

Murphy, Murphy and Newcomb (1937) came to the conclusion that there was no significant relationship between susceptibility to persuasion and mental age or intelligence. Subsequent work of Hovland and Janis (1959), Hovland, Janis and Kelly (1953) also felled to find appreciable relation-ships between susceptibility and intelligence.

Stukat (1958) gave a battery of 22 suggestibility tests to 11 year old school girls whose intelligence-test scores were known. There was a negative correlation between intelligence and suggestibility on 17 of those tests, 10 reaching conventional level of significance while none of the 5 positive correlations was significant. The same researcher gave 17 suggestibility teats to young adults in their 20's and found that 12 correlated negatively with intelligence (5 significantly) while none of the 4 positively correlations was significant.

(viii) Self esteem and attitude change

Berkowitz and Lundy (1957), Cohen (1959), Hochbaum (1954), Janis (1954), Kelman (1950), Mausner (1954), and Maus-ner and Mausner (1955) reported studies that showed negative relationship between self-esteem and influenceability whereas positive or non-monotonic relation- ship was reported by Cox and Bauer (1964), Gelfand (1962), Gollob and Ditties (1965), Leventhal and Perloe (1962), Silverman (1964), Silverman, Ford and Morganti (1966).

(ix) Sex and attitude

Stukat (1958) and Weitzenhoffer (1953) found that females are more susceptible than males, in their studies on suggestibility in social influence situations. Females conform more than males, according to studies by King (1956). Females are more persuadable than males, as found in the studies of Janis and Field (1959) and Knower (1936).

Ableson and Lesser (1959), Beloff (1958), Hilgard, (1965), Janis and Field (1959), King (1956) and Lesser and Ableson (1970), concluded that individual difference variables predict influenceability more strongly for males than females. An exception to these findings was that of Barber and Calverley (1964).

Eagly's (1975) study on sex-difference and influence ability found little evidence for the oft-cited tendency for females to be more easily influenced than males, except in group pressure conformity situations modeled after the Asch and Sherif situations.

Tuthill and Forsyth (1962) in attempting a self-presentational interpretation of persuasiveness, measured attitudes of 48 male and 50 female undergraduate students, before and after a direct persuasion attempt. Reports of attitude change supported Eagle's findings, since females, when the need to manage impressions was high, made greater use of opinion conformity in their self-presentations, while males' self presentations included instances of opinion conformity, independence and dissent.

2.4.5 Destination factors

(i) Type of issue and attitude change

Mc Garvey (1943) in his experiment concerning social prestige of various occupations, concluded that judgments of persons are determined not only by the properties of the object perceived but also by a supplied frame of reference which serves to determine whether the object is related to increase or decrease of drive. Hence, it also determines the nature of the attitude.

Peak (1955) directed a programme of research on attitude change and concluded that attitude change results from expected satisfaction from goals served by an attitude or changes in the instrumental relations believed to exist between the attitude object and the goal.

The impact on participants of a pre-retirement seminar was studied by Shoukasmith (1983), by assessing the concept of retirement on a set of semantic differential scales at pre and post-course sessions. Attitude change, when it occurred, was in the direction of perceiving retirement as a more active concept in participants' lives and in increasing its positive evaluation from an initial low point.

(ii) Temporal decay of induced attitude change

The persistence of induced attitude change was studied by a number of researchers Annis and Mier (1934) found that the originally induced opinion change was retained as long as four months, or even ten months. At the other end there are studies which show practically no remnant of the initially induced opinion change after six months (Chen, 1936; Eberhard and Bauer, 1941; Sims, 1938) Petersen and Thurstone (1933) reported both the extremes within a single study on the persistence of opinion change induced by a series of commercial picture films. Cherrigton and Miller (1933), Hall (1938) opined that the attitude change induced by the 'typical' persuasive communication has a half-life of about six months. Dietrich (1946) and Mc Guire (1957) found that about 40% of the initially induced change had decayed after one week and Walts and Mc Guire (1964) found that about 60% decay took place in six weeks.

Studies of Laventhal, Jones and Trembly (1966), Laventhal, Watts and Pagano (1967) on fear arousal and attitude change, suggested that long term behaviour change is a function of two distinct components: knowledge of danger (a cognitive factor) and an action structure. They maintained that neither an attitude nor a change in attitude necessarily leads to a behaviour or to a change in behaviour. As Doob (1947) suggested that connecting attitude to action seems to involve a process which is separate from that of changing attitudes only and the experiments suggest that this connection requires, what Cartwright (1949) called, an 'action structure'.

(iii) Verbal opinion changes vs gross action changes

The works of Calder, Ross and Insko (1973), Cooper and Worchel (1970) utilizing the Festinger and Carlsmith (1959) paradigm showed that dissonance effect occurs only when the attitude discrepant behaviour leads to aversive or unwanted consequence.

Cooper and Worchel (1970), Cooper, Zanna and Goethals (1975) found that attitude change occurred if subjects expected that their counter-attitudinal essays definitely or even possibly would result in unwarranted consequences, and they expected no information about whether the consequences occurred.

Pallak, Sogin and Van Zante (1974) examined forcibility in studies involving negative consequences of finding out that the task is trivial and worthless. The result proved that, while forcibility typically increases personal responsibility for consequences, it is not crucial for obtaining attitude change if other cues (e.g., high choice) cause subjects to assume responsibility for negative consequences.

In the study of Reiss and Schlenker (1977), they forced subjects to make a counter attitudinal speech that produced aversive consequences, attitude change occurred only when the subjects were given high choice to engage in the act and, after the speech a majority of observers who were present gave subjects feedback attributing high decision- freedom to them.

2.5 STUDIES ON ATTITUDE CHANGES IN TEACHERS AND STUDENTS

2.5.1. Teacher attitudes

Scott and Brinkley (1960) found a slight degree of association between attitude change of student teachers and the attitudes of their supervising teachers. The conclusion, that during student teaching, significant changes occurred in a negative direction in attitude toward children on the MTAI. Both highly anxious and non-anxious student teachers had both negative changes in attitudes in the direction of those of the regular teaching staff. A change in attitude in the direction of that of the supervising teachers has been demonstrated by Johnson (1968) too in America.

In India, Verma (1968) found that teacher training had neither improved nor reduced the social values of the trainees. The pact of teacher training programme on the attitude of student teachers toward children and schoolwork had been consistently favorable. It was found that attitudes ware not significantly related to their theoretical, economic, aesthetic and religious values. The student- teachers' attitudes toward the curriculum were related to the values they held and the values held by their staff members. Age was found to be a significant variable only in respect of general values: older teachers tended to hold more traditional values, but the level of education contributed to the conflicts in educational values, persons of higher education expressing more progressive values and vice versa.

Mazer (1969) in his study on those who had just completed the undergraduate elementary teacher education course, concluded that attitudes and personal values of student teachers could be significantly modified appropriate to their work to deal with disadvantaged youth, through 'training'.

Kakkar (1970) determined the influence of teacher training upon the attitude of undergraduate students toward children. (N =160 Elementary Teacher Trainees, Tool: MTAI). The findings were that (i) the attitudes of teacher trainees, when considered as one group, did change in the direction of more liberal attitudes towards children during the teacher training programmes, (ii) actual teaching, including first hand experience with children, was the most conducive to such change in attitudes, observing children and observing teachers' interacting with children in the classroom (the former more than the latter) followed.

Kennedy and Humphrey (1971) attempted to find the effect of training in the systems approach upon changing pre-service teacher attitudes toward the seven instructional design factors selected. Significant differences were reported between the experimental and control groups in evaluative ratings for 6 of the 7 factors. The conclusion was, that, systems approach concepts could affect pre--service teachers' attitudes from a teacher-oriented to learner-oriented instructional environment.

Langenbac (1972) found that teachers could be differentiated on the basis of their attitudes toward curriculum use and planning by means of the Curriculum Attitude Inventory (CAI). Teachers with curriculum planning experience had more positive attitudes towards curriculum use and planning than teachers without such experience, but not totally irrespective of grade and experience levels.

Studies of Singh (1979), Singh and Sharma (1977) revealed that there were significant relationship between attitude toward teaching and indirectness of classroom verbal interaction of student teachers (Flanders' system).

Kamla Bhutani (1977) examined the effects of cognitive consistency, cognitive complexity and personality rigidity on attitude change. In addition to these, the relationship of sex, radicalism-conservatism and extremeness to attitude change were also studied (N = 1290 college students; tools: Radicalism-conservatism scale, Milton Rokeash's Narrow-mindedness Test, Rigidity scale). The findings were that (i) cognitively consistent subjects were more resistant ones, (ii) subjects having cognitively complex system were more prone to change than those having simple cognitive system, (iii) rigid subjects were more immune to change than the non-rigid ones, (iv) subjects having extreme attitudes with regard to MM Scale were less prone to changes, (v) girls were more amenable to persuasion than boys (though the difference was not highly significant).

Simonson (1977) conducted an experiment on 218 subjects using the Media Education Attitude scale. The conclusion was that the subjects with negative attitudes toward the content of a teacher education course in media- methods significantly proved in attitudes after treatment procedures. The subjects with positive attitudes toward the content achieved significantly better than those with negative initial attitudes.

Ahluwalia (1978) attempted to identify the nature and extent of change in professional attitudes of student teachers resulting from training for one academic year (N = 648 student teachers. Tool: Teacher Attitude Inventory developed by the researcher himself). He found that (i) The changes in attitudes were, to some extent, deter-mined by the type of institutions attended by a particular group, (ii) The results of the total group indicated change in the negative direction in the professional. Attitudes of student teachers on four of the six sub-scales. (iii) the differences in mean attitude scores of male and female student teachers were non significant in all except one case.

Yesodhara (1979) tried to assess the direction and attitude of attitude changes achieved through the teacher education programme (one year B.Ed,. course). She found that attitudes to teaching as a profession, pupils, school work and professional growth changed significantly in the desired direction (more positive) in the large group as a whole, and in each Institutional group, though there were clear institutional differences in the magnitude of change.

Riohardson (1981) investigated whether any change of attitude toward teacher participation in school decision making occurs among student teachers between the completion of their college course and the end of their probationary years. 175 subjects completed questionnaire consisting of 8 decision scales in 1974 and again in 1975. At the end of the probationary year, the responses to the same item statements were less democratically and less liberally oriented toward teacher participation in school decision making.

Klingman (1982) used a role-stimulation model. To test a 4-phase role-stimulation model; 33 elementary school teachers attended a stimulation programme, 32 attended a lecture and 30 others served as a control group. All the subjects were assessed on attitudes toward and actual behaviours in 5 stress-related activities one week before, intervention and seven weeks later. It was found that relative to other subjects, subjects in the stimulation group shifted more toward positive attitudes in their class- rooms and attempted more behavioural activities with regard to anticipatory preparation to potential crisis.

Susana d Souza Barros and Marcos F. Elia (1998) conducted a study entitled "Physics teacher's attitudes: how do they affect the reality of the classroom and models for change?" from: Connecting Research in Physics Education with Teacher Education ·An I.C.P.E. Book International

Commission on Physics Education 1997 and 1998. So, it was concluded that there are no universal methods to modify this situation. That is, there are a variety of science teaching styles as a result of the strong interaction existing between teaching attitudes and competencies, school and society.

Uzunboylu, Huseyin (2007) conducted a study entitled "Teacher attitudes toward online education following an online in-service program". This study sought to determine attitudes toward online education of English language teachers. Following the program, significant differences in attitude toward online education were found.

2.5.2 Student attitudes

Janet T. Spence, Eugene D. Hahn (1997) conducted a study entitled "the attitudes toward women scale and attitude change in college students "to determine cohort changes in gender-role attitudes, responses to the 15-item form of the attitudes toward women scale were compared for students at the same university tested in 1972, 1976, 1980, and 1992. In both males and females, members of the 1992 cohort were the most egalitarian, and members of the 1972 cohort were the least egalitarian. In all groups, women were significantly less traditional in their attitudes than men. As has been found in previous studies, detailed analyses of the data from the 1992 cohort revealed that the scale was unifactorial, but that the score distributions were skewed. There was also some indication of ceiling effects at the egalitarian end of the scale, particularly in women.

Twist, L. et al. (2004) conducted a study "Good readers but at a cost? Attitudes towards reading in England". The major objective of the study is to find change in attitudes towards reading in England. A review of the results of selected surveys over the past 30 years suggests that there may be some evidence of attitudes to reading in primary schools becoming less positive.

Sainsbury, M. & Schagen. I. (2004) conducted a study entitled "attitudes towards reading at ages nine to eleven", and concluded that changes may be related to the introduction of the national literacy strategy, but other explanations are also possible.

2.6 SUMMING UP

Some of the general conclusions from the studies reviewed are:

1) parents of low and lower middle-class strata of SES tend to instill in their children the importance of residence and acceptance of status and authority, while the upper-middle class parents encourage

high aspirations and non-acceptant attitude toward existing pattern of conditions, in their children,

2) the resentment against caste system is very much higher in south India than in north. India and a majority of youngsters do not favour inter-caste marriages,

3) student attitudes toward careers could be changed by exposure to career information containing non-traditional role models,

4) students with more than average achievement have generally more socially acceptable attitudes than average and below average students,

5) group conformity and pressures foster liberal attitudes whereas ego-defensiveness seems to lead to conservatism,

6) in studying attitude change situations it is important to measure not only valence but also intensity of attitudes,

7) girls/women seem to be generally more susceptible to persuasion than boys/men - but not in all cases,

8) children around 8-9 years seem to be most suggestible, suggestibility then declines till the end of adolescence and then levels off, and

9) attitude change shows an internal decline Boon after the persuasive message, and then a gradual, steady decline over a few weeks, till it stabilizes at a certain level.

Further, attitude change seems to be facilitated by 1) high credibility sources/messages more than low credibility ones, 2) explicit statement of conclusions (at the beginning or end of message) by the communicator, more than implicit ones left to be drawn by the recipients, 3) role playing, if the public expression of view different from one's private view is rewarded, 4) the recipient's dislike for the person advocating the new position (under certain conditions), 5) the emotion eliciting qualities of the communicator, 6) threats rather than severe threats, under certain conditions conducive to long-term internalization of change, 7) the recipient being put in pleasant mood, by 8) the immediacy with which arguments follow expression of opinion (and vice versa), 9) well organized (structured) messages that facilitate comprehension and carry conviction, rather than disorganized ones that lower source evaluation, 10) refuting the opposite view, rather than ignoring it (especially in the case of an intelligent group), 11) agreeable-to-disagreeable' order of points or arguments, 12) learning, playing a significant role in mediating source-persuasion relationship, 13) regency of message, rather than its primacy, 14) unexpected communications, 15) the message taking a position of moderate discrepancy - rather than an extreme/opposite view - from the recipient's initial position, 16) verbal clues rather than visual clues, 17) live or video messages more than audio-taped messages, and that more than written messages, 18) written message/modality rather than oral one (facilitating comprehension) when the matter' is difficult to understand, 19) 'message set' rather than 'task set, as the former tends to reduce counter-argumentation while the latter aids devaluation of communication, 20) group discussion and decision, rather than lecture, especially when a consensus is sought, though group- listening followed by free discussion might counteract the effect of a persuasive communication in the event of a division of opinion in the group, 21) asking the subject to make an 'improvised speech' rather than reading a prepared one, 22) increasing the salience of initial attitudes, 23) dispositional attributions, 24) expected satisfaction from goals apposed to be served by an attitude or the change and 25) group pressures and conformity, strengthened by the length of affiliation to the group.

Rao P.S. (1984) concluded that many of the above findings are complementary and consistent; the results of the studies are not very conclusive. Especially in the case of relationship between individual difference factors like sex, SES and family background and attitude change, and the relative effective-ness of different forms or models of communication like oral and written communication, audio- visual and dramatized communication and attitude change - indicating ample scope for further research in this area. Further, most of the studies were conducted in laboratory type controlled situations, in a normal school setting, in such a way that, the treatments, with the messages and materials, could be absorbed into the regular educational programme.

2.7 CONCLUSION

In the chapter entitled "Review of related literature" is related to survey of attitudes more specifically general social attitudes, teacher attitudes, student attitudes, and also related to attitude development more specifically longitudinal studies, cross sectional studies in attitude development and changes. It is also subjected to the literature related to changing attitudes more specially source factors, attractiveness of communicator, mild vs severe threat and attitude change, power and attitude change and source valence and attitude change. It is also related to discrepancy and attitude change more specifically about channel factors: medium of communication and attitude change, mass media effectiveness in attitude change, distraction and attitude change and group discussion vs lecture and attitude change. It is related to receiver factors in attitude change more specifically active participation and attitude change, role playing and attitude change, predispositions of message recipient and attitude change, compliance and attitude change, self attribution process and attitude change etc.

So, the present study is an attempt based on the above presented information to test the relative effective-ness of three different communication strategies suitable for a normal classroom setting in changing the attitudes of special relevance and their retention.

CHAPTER 3

DESIGN OF THE STUDY

The study was conceived as an experimental study aimed at finding the effectiveness of the three treatments, viz., verbal-visual communication strategy (T_1), dramatized-multimedia communication strategy (T_2) and Integrated of these two strategies (T_3), in producing change in the desired direction in three attitudes of the students studying IX class in Secondary Schools. It also aimed at finding the differences by sex and socio-economic status (SES), religion and rural, urban in respect of the initial position on the three attitudes and change achieved in them through the treatment.

3.1 OBJECTIVES OF THE STUDY

The specific objectives of the present study could be defined as follows:

a) To assess the attitude differences by sex, SES, demographic area (rural & urban), caste and religion sub groups among secondary school children ;

b) To develop detailed teaching strategies, plans and materials for the following educational treatments:

   i. Verbal-visual communication - in different forms like talks, discussion, written materials, visual materials and self – instructional materials.

   ii. Dramatized-multimedia which might be include of situational filmstrips of different films in Telugu language movies.

   iii. A combination of verbal-visual and dramatized-multimedia communication methods in (i) and (ii).

c) To find out the change in attitude in the desired direction obtained from the above programme.

d) To make a comparative study of the effect the treatments in producing the attitude change.

e) To study the retentivity of the attitude change produced if any, after a period of six months vis-a-vis the treatments and the three attitudes.

3.2. HYPOTHESES

The hypotheses formulated for verification were:

H-I

(i) Each of the educational treatments employing different communication strategies (verbal-visual and dramatized-multimedia communication and Intergraded) will produce significant change in the desired direction in respect of the attitudes towards manual work, casteism, family planning and

(ii) The attitude change thus produced will be retained after a period of six months.

H-II

(i) There will be no significant differences between the three treatments in respect of the direction and magnitude of change produced in the attitudes concerned and

(ii) Its retention after a period of six months.

H-III

(i) There will be no significant difference between (I) boys and girls, (II) students belonging to different socioeconomic status (SES) (III) demographic sub groups, (IV) caste, (V) religion, (VI) parental qualification in respect of the changes produced in them by the different treatments and

(ii) Its retention after a period of six months.

3.3 DEFINITIONS OF OPERATIONAL TERMS

(A) Attitude

It is a fairly stable mental disposition towards psychological objects such as persons, ideas, objects, institutions, and situations in the environment, based on one's experiences and involving predictable responses to anticipated situations.

(B) Attitude change

Attitude change is any alteration in the direction, degree, or intensity of an attitude. A change in one component of a given attitude may produce change in other components.

C) Manual work

Following the deflnition given in the oxford Dictionary, it is considered as 'work done with hands (labor)', more broadly as work involving physical effort or labor but not of the kind required in the professions.

(D) Casteism

According to Oxford Dictionary castes are hereditary classes with members practicing certain rites and trades and shunning social intercourse with other classes. For the purpose of this study, casteism, is considered as a prejudice which is a primary attitude shared by group as a whole in a society in which an individual is not judged as individual, he is rather judged as a member of caste group based on his parentage. Casteism also implies.

I. Perceptions of divisions, hereditary and relationships based,

II. Acceptance, bias, preferences, favours, promotion of interests, etc. in respect of one's caste, and

III. Prejudice, indifference, dislike, rejection, disfavour, antagonism, obstruction, etc. in respect of other castes.

(E) Family planning

It is a planning of one's family in order to control its growth and size with 'a small norm'.

(F) Retentivity

According to Oxford Dictionary retentivity means effective in retaining facts and impressions (of a person's memory)

(G) Socio-economic-status

As suggested by Prof. Singh R. A. and Saxena (1981), it is the status of an Individual in the society as determined by the three variables: occupation, education and income. In this study, however, these variables refer to those of the parents of the students.

(H) Verbal-visual communication

All communications through the medium of language (spoken or written form) is verbal; it may consist in talks, discussions, interactions, presentation of written materials etc. and demand aural-oral or reading comprehension. By visual communication is meant presentation of ideas or messages through two-dimensional graphic materials like charts and cartoons, or through three-dimensional presentations; however visual media in this project were limited to pictures and charts.

(I) Dramatized -multimedia communication

This is essentially an emotionally charged, enacted presentation, involving characters, role playing, acting, etc., and employing verbal and non-verbal communications, especially, expressions, gestures, postures and movements, and non-verbal sounds. Direct effective appeal is intended, apart from cognitive communication with affective contention the broad sense it is audio-visual communication employing human characters and agents in the context of a structured theme, plot or story. It may take the form of story telling (with emphasis on feelings, expressions, gestures, etc.), mono acting, skits, playlets, play, dance-drama, movie (film/film strips from different movies), etc.

Dramatized multimedia is the use of different *media* to convey *information*; *text* together with *audio, graphics* and *animation*, often *packaged* on *CD-ROM*/DVD.

3.4 VARIABLES IN THE STUDY

In the present study, the independent variables are the communication strategy employed in effecting attitude change and it took three treatment forms as mentioned above, while the three attitudes – those towards manual work, casteism and family planning – formed the dependent variables. Other variables like time interval, essential content and length of the treatment and source were controlled by making them uniform for all the groups, so that the effect of variables become neutral. The recipient variables were also adequately controlled by systematic sampling technique and a rotation design. Sex, socio-economic status (SES), demographic sub groups (rural and urban, caste, religion, and parental qualifications, were taken as predictor variables in relation to the criteria of initial position and change achieved in respect of dependent variables those are attitudes.

3.5 TECHNIQUES OF MEASUREMENT AND TOOL DEVELOPMENT

3.5.1 Techniques and tools

The independent variable was communication strategies, which was manipulated and varies in two ways which are in sets of activities did not require any measurement. The dependent variables had to be measured with validity and precision by three attitude scales, which were to be developed and standardized earlier by Dr. P.S. Rao in 1982, and they are:

VISAM scale: Visakha student attitude toward manual work scale

VISAC scale: Visakha student attitude toward casteism scale

VISAF scale: Visakha student attitude toward family planning scale

The same scale is used for pre-test, post-test-1 and post-test-2. The predictor variable of SES were based on the scale Prof. Singh. R.A. and Prof. S.K. Saxena scale (1981), vide Appendix 'C'.

3.5.2 Attitude Scale developments and validation

3.5.2.1 Techniques for measuring attitudes

The most direct approach to the measurement of attitudes is, simply, to ask people in one manner or other, what their attitudes are. Haire (1950) found that attitudes were not so easily or satisfactorily detected through direct questioning. Self-report inventories with measurement 'on an internal scale are called attitude scales' and much of the literature on the measurement of attitudes concerns different methods of developing such attitude scales. Projective techniques like projecting TAT-type pictures, eliciting stories have also been employed real or non--real behaviour indicating the degree to which one would be willing to participate in the activities concerned was also explored as a measure of attitudes (Campbell, 1950; Cook and Sellitz, 1964).

The purpose of an attitude scale is to assign an, individual to a position somewhere between the opposite extremes of favoring or opposing some thing. This position may be defined, with reference to one dimension or more. A few of such single-dimension methods attempted are measuring social distance (Bogardus, 1928), method of equal appearing intervals (Thurstone and Chave, 1929) and methods which take in to account-range, consistency and intensity of attitude response (Likert, 1932).

The deterministic model that has received wide attention for the scaling of verbalized attitudes is the monotone deterministic model which is usually referred to as 'Guttman scale' (developed by Guttman, 1950). In this model it is hypothesized that each dichotomous item has a perfect bi-serial correlation with the hypothesized trait. Thurstone scale is a non-monotone probability model. This method employs judges to establish scale values for items. In a typical study judges would rate the attitude implied by each of the 100 statements. The judgments could be made on 11-step continuum ranging from 'strongly positive' to 'strongly negative' attitude. The median rating by the judges is the scale value of that statement. About 20 items are selected for the final scale.

In the summative model of Likert, it is assumed that individual items are monotonically related to the underlying traits and that a summation of item scores is approximately linear-related to the trait. The total scale consists in a number of statements, positive (favorable) and negative (unfavorable) ones in more or less equal number and in a random, unsystematic order, requiring the subject to express his opinion or judgment usually on a five point scale, ranging from strongly agree to strongly disagree. These summative Likert scales have a number of attractive advantages over the other models because (1) they follow an appealing model, (2) they are rather easy to construct, (3) they are usually highly reliable, (4) they can be adapted to the measurement of different kinds of attitudes, and (5) they have produced meaningful results in many studies to date, and they have been shown to be as efficacious as Thrustone's complicated model (Nunnally, 1970).

Edward and Kilpatrick (1948) developed a method called, 'the scale-discrimination technique', in an attempt to systematize the scale construction by Thrustone, Likert and Guttman.

Hammond (1948) developed a disguised test of attitudes in his 'error-choice technique'. He forced subjects to choose between two alternative answers to questions, each answer being equally wrong, but in opposite directions from the correct answer.

Stephenson (1953) developed the Q-sort, for studying verbalized attitudes, self-description, preferences, etc. It requires the respondent to sort out large number of statements as relevant to/true of him or not.

Osgood (1962) developed a technique for measuring the connotative meaning of concepts by getting ratings on a bipolar adjective scales (usually seven point scales) called "semantic differential". This technique also has been applied 'to the measurement of attitudes.'

De Weiss, Susan, Jones and David (1981) reported a study using several attitude scales and questionnaires with various response formats (multiple choice, Likert Scales). It was observed that many subjects ignored the response format and expressed their opinions in their own words. Lower Class women showed a greater number of contradictions and more disregard for specific instructions than middle class women, when asked to respond to multiple choice and close-end questions than they did in unstructured inter views and when responding to open-end questions. Pilot projects to determine the range and format of questions to be used were advised in such cases.

Among the different techniques reviewed here, the Likert technique continues to be the most popular, for the reasons quoted above.

3.5.2.2 Validation of attitude scales

Gulliksen (1950) suggested that if a scale measured a representative sample of all the beliefs, feelings, and action-tendencies pertaining to an object, the scale could be taken to have good 'content validity'. He argued that this is the reason why Thrustone and Likert collected a very large number of heterogeneous items presumably touching on all the main kinds of beliefs and feelings about the attitude under consideration. Another method of validation is by measurement of 'known groups' as done by Sims (1938).

Overt behaviour as a validation criterion for attitude measurement, Murphy, Murphy and Newcomb (1937). But Guilford (1959) observed that a verbalized attitude might not correlate highly with behaviour pertaining to the attitude. This does not necessarily mean, however, that verbalized attitudes are invalid, as pointed out by Nunnally Jr (1970)

Katz and Stotland (1959) concluded that only 'balanced, attitudes' would seem to be characterized by high consistency.

A good attitude scale should have (i) construct validity in terms of aspects covered under attitude as defined/understood, (ii) content validity in terms of relevance to the object of the attitude, and (iii) empirical validity established statistically in terms of internal consistency, discrimination between (nominated) extreme groups, high correlation with a validated tool measuring the same attitude, etc. Pilot studies are usually conducted for item validation and selection (based on internal consistency/ discrimination between top and bottom groups) and for establishing the validity and reliability of the whole scale in its final form.

3.6 STANDARDIZATION OF TOOLS

The above tool is adopted and conducted pilot study of 400 students in each attitude for IX standard students of four co-educational high schools in Visakhapatnam city.

The aim of the study was to determine whether the test items intended to measure the same variable were measuring something in common and to test whether the items possessed the desired qualities of measurement, especially discrimination. In other words, items were to be analyzed for discriminative power and internal consistency. Then responses were scored and the summated scores were arranged in the descending order for about 370 students (dropping a few cases of obvious indifference); the top and bottom 27 % of the total of 370, that is 100 each, were used to carry out item analysis. The discriminatory power of each item was determined by calculating the "X" value for each item as suggested by Garrett (1958). Statements whose X^2 values were greater than 13.277 (the value of 'X' or significance at 1% level for 4 d.f.) were selected. It was ensured that the numbers of positive and negative statements were more or less equal in each scale after the item analysis and selection, and they were arranged without any perceptive pattern. Also statements that were related to each other or similar to each other were placed at some distance from each other. Thus emerged the final forms (vide Appendix A for items and their x^2 values of discrimination and the printed Telugu version which was actually used). These scales were translated into Telugu language with the help of language specialists and schoolteachers. They were administered to an adequate representative sample of 400 students for validation purposes. Coefficients of reliability were calculated by the split-half method and found to be very high (given in Table 1). The whole scale could not be validated further through concurrence with an accepted tool measuring the same variable (there were none) or through. Discrimination between nominated extreme groups (there was no valid basis or evidence for such nomination). Thus while content validity and construct validity were built up through the efforts detailed above, empirical validity was ensured only through internal consultancy and the discriminative power of the items.

3.6.1 Construction and standardization of tools

Likert's method of summated ratings was followed in constructing the three attitude scales. At first 50 items were constructed (25 positively directed and an equal number negatively directed) in respect of each attitude under consideration, after consulting experienced people in the field of education and psychology. Care was taken to see all aspects of the attitudes concerned were included and each statement expresses a favorable/unfavorable opinion on the subject. As suggested by Wang (1932), Thrustone and Chave (1929), and Edwards and Kilpatrick (1948), the following criteria were followed as in construction and tenderization of tools:

i. Statements that referred to the past or factual position or that could be interpreted in more. Than one way or that was irrelevant were avoided.

ii. Statements that were selected to cover entire range of aspects regarding the attitudes under consideration, as analyzed.

iii. The language of each statement was kept clear and direct, and only such yards were used as could be expected to be familiar to IX standard students.

iv. Statements were short and crisp without ambiguity.

v. Each Statement contained one and only one complete thought.

vi. Double barreled statements, double negatives, etc., were avoided.

vii. Each statement not only had content relevant to the attitude but also could be clearly defined as positive or negative.

After a careful scrutiny and discussion by a group of experienced persons, the items were accepted; rejected or redefined. The preliminary farms as made out had 40 items each. The positive and negative items were arranged in a jumbled order without any pattern, with items having similar or closely related content, at different positions. Provision was made for expressing agreement or disagreement to each item on a five-point scale [Strongly Agree (A) Agree (B) - Neutral (C) - Disagree (D) - Strongly Disagree (E)] and for scoring the responses of positive and negative items with weights of 5,4,3, 2, 1 and 1,2,3,4,5 respectively summated ratings was followed in constructing the three attitude scales in Likert's method, as suggested by Tuckman (1972) and De Weiss et al. (1981.

Garrett (1958) opinions that the validation of content through competent judgments is most satisfactory when the sampling of items is wide and judicious and when adequate standardization groups are utilized. In the present case both the above criteria were satisfied and the three scales have content validity and construct validity. More over the validity index of each item (its discriminating power) was determined and the internal consistency of all the items in each scale was established. Fine details of number of positive and negative items, average X^2 value of discrimination of the items, and reliability coefficient are given below - vide Table 1.

Table 1: Validity and reliability attitude scales

Number of items	Scales		
	VISAM scale	VISAC scale	VISAF Scale
Positive	15	15	14
Negative	15	15	14
Total	30	30	28
Average value of X^2 discrimination	40.128	30.753	48.948
Split half reliability coefficient	0.848	0.909	0.907

1.7 THE EXPERIMENTAL TREATMENTS

3.7.1 General principles and strategies

Attitudes could be changed through

i. Direct experience of the attitudinal object or situation.
ii. Effective communication or message altering the relevant cognitive structures and accompanying feelings.
iii. Encouraging a person to behave in ways consistent with the desired change in attitudes.

iv. Providing positive reinforcement, among other things, of this communication would be the most economical and the one most convenient for school-type educational setting. Once the source is selected and the essence of the message decided the choice available could be mainly in respect of channel factors: media, modes and materials of communication.

Hovland, Janis and Kelly (1953), and Mc Guire (1968) described a series of steps characterizing an attitude change Process:

Stimuli → Attention → Comprehension → Yielding → Retention → Action (response).

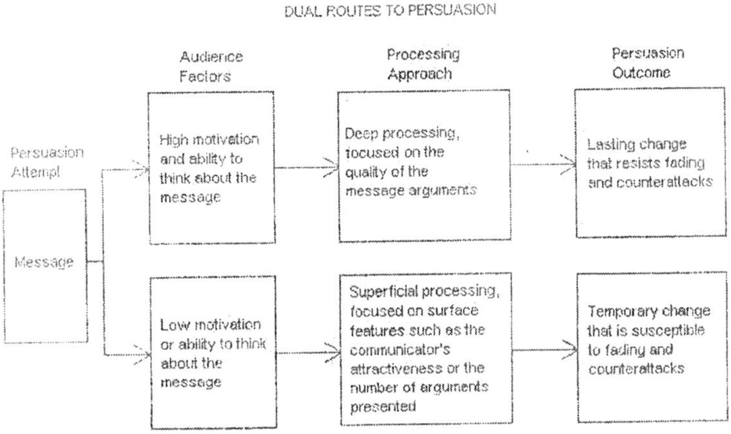

DUAL ROUTES TO PERSUASION

Persuasion Attempt
Message
Audience Factors
High motivation and ability to think about the message
Low motivation or ability to think about the message
Processing Approach
Deep processing, focused on the quality of the message arguments
Superficial processing, focused on surface features such as the communicator's attractiveness or the number of arguments presented
Persuasion Outcome
Lasting change that resists fading and counterattacks
Temporary change that is susceptible to fading and counterattacks

(**Source:** *http://chiron.valdosta.edu/mawhately/767/attitude.htm*)

Like in any communication in this study also situation all the target subjects might not pay attention to the stimuli presented, not all those who receive and register the stimuli might understand the message fully, not all those who understood, it might yield to the message, and only some of these who accept it might remember long enough and still less number might care to do any thing about it. Communication must be so planned, structured, and presented as to compel attention. Ensure reasonable compre-hension (with appropriate control of language and representa-tion), persuade acceptance and compliance, and facilitate good retention and encourage appropriate behaviour, which would imply the intended change. Communication in school-type situations is largely verbal - spoken or written. Supporting and supplementing (not necessarily substituting) verbal communication with audio-visual presentation (as aids at least) has been emphasized as a productive principle in education and has been found to be of value. Visual aids may be two-dimen-sional or three-dimensional; recorded -presentations can, not only take 'natural sounds' into any situation bat effectively present spoken messages - discussed or audiovisual presentation. Audiovisual aids (video presentation) itself has been generally emphasized in education as a powerful medium for cognitive communication and direct affective appeal, with good effect. Visual aids, audiovisual and dramatized-multimedia aids (recorded video with cinema clippings) are also accepted as capable of sustaining student interest. In a laboratory-type situation the choice the question of comparison could be between lecture and discussion, audio and visual presentations, oral and written forms, instruction and audiovisual and dramatized-multimedia aids (recorded video with cinema clippings), video presentation by others and role playing by the subjects, etc. But in a school-type setting many of these could be taken in meaning-ful and feasible Integrated, though activities like dramatized-multimedia would require special skills, arrangements and efforts like scripts, choreography, setting and facilities, rehearsal and direction, apart from a team of persons with talent in the field.

It was therefore considered appropriate to plan and try out three composite strategies of communication – one mainly with forms/modes commonly used in schools, one mainly with special forms/modes of dramatized-multimedia aids (recorded video with cinema clippings), and a third combining the two; they were selected, labeled and defined as follows, each consisting of four types of presentations:

T_1 : The verbal-visual communication strategy consists of

Sl.No	Communication strategy	Consisting form
1	Talk	Spoken form
2	Panel discussion	
3	Self instructional material	Written form
4	Reading material plus comprehension questions	

Sl.No	Communication strategy	Consisting form
1	Mono-acting	With gestures, and Expressions
2	Play –let	With gestures, Expressions,
3	Skit	Dialogue, gestures, And Expressions,
4	Dramatized-multimedia aid	Recorded video with cinema clippings

Slno	Communication strategy	Consisting form
1	Mono-acting	With gestures, Expressions,
2	Dramatized -multimedia aid	Recorded video with cinema clippings
3	Self instructional material	Written form
4	Reading material Plus comprehension questions	

It was also accepted in principle that the themes and essential content covered in the different forms of presentation under the two strategies would be the same, though the details might vary to some extent

3.8 DRAMATISED MULTIMEDIA STRATEGY

3.8.1 Verbal-visual Communication Strategy (T_1)

In the talk and panel discussion presentations, the communicator/ communicators would put across, to the group of students selected; the points intended to be communicated with a brief introduction suitable to establish rapport and to create interest. The essence or conclusion of the message would also be indicated/highlighted at the beginning or end of each unit of communication. Further, some active inter- discussion was also provided for after the presentation. The students would be very familiar with these forms of communication in their classroom and school situations and on the radio, this should facilitate easy compression. Moreover, research findings seemed to indicate, though not conclusively, that group discussion rather than lecture would be more interesting and persuasive. But the group discussion method, if employed in different schools without adequate training and rehearsal would result in variation in the communicator variable, it would be difficult to control certain variables of content and channel as well. So instead of group discussion by the students themselves, a group of specially trained people put up a uniform panel discussion after adequate rehearsals before the group concerned in the schools, however some interaction with the group was added.

Self-instructional materials were included because it would allow and require active interaction between each student and the message content and permit each student to study the material at his own pace for the sake of maximum comprehension. File salient points would be reviewed, integrated and highlighted at the end through an interactive discussion.

A more familiar type of silent reading exercise followed by reasoning and interactive discussion based on compression questions of the types used in language courses was also employed to facilitate active learning and adequate comprehension of the message. The subjects would read the passage at his own pace and writes answers to the questions that followed, in the space provided. In the end the communicator would read the questions one by one, confirm the answers and correct the incorrect answers and discuss doubts and clarification by eliciting the relevant points and arguments from those who had answered correctly, and in doing so, automatically summaries the salient points. A brief description of the talks, panel discussions, reading passages, and self-instructional materials and illustrations of the latter are given in Appendix B.

3.8.2 Dramatized multimedia communication (film strips) strategy (T_2)

(i) **Mono acting:** This also form a very common and favorite item in most of the school entertainment programme. This goes beyond story telling in that one actor enacts the deference (a few) roles, with action and expression, as appropriate, apart from dialogue delivery. Dramatization as a dimension of the presentation is stranger than that in story telling. Moreover, on of the members of the team that assisted the investigator had got good experience on the stage as a mono-acting specialist and with that confidence that it could be made effective it was include in both T_2 and T_3.

(ii) **Skits :** These were included in T_2, because adolescent boys and girls are in a position to enjoy the subtle wit and sarcasm which is a distinguishing characteristic of a skit - especially of the social maladies of the contemporary society. It has heavier dramatized-multimedia than mono-acting in that different actors play the different roles and there is greater emphasis on effective communication and appeal through the powerful dialogue, symbolization, other representations and humor. Here also enough caution was exercised to ensure that the theme was familiar and the message was presented in a fairly 'direct' way.

(iii) **Playlets:** These were included in T_2 because it is usual for schools and other agencies to present this for as socially educative entertainment. It would be longer than skits, with more characters and more intricate plot. It is a shortened or abridged version of a full play-like one act plays. It can have appropriate theme and message, which could be conveyed with could be conveyed with intense drama, elegance of appeal.

(iv) **Dramatized multimedia (video recorded with movie strips show):** The investigator made three, 45 minute video film CD on the theme of manual work, casteism and family planning and emphasizing the message of manual work, casteism, small family. Skits, mono-acting and playlets were specially planned were appropriate theme content and message in relation to the three attitudes. Done well, these should make a powerful impact on impressionable minds and sustain their interest, and above all effective substantial attitude change.

3.8.3. *Integrated communication strategy (T3)*

As pointed out earlier in this chapter, this treatment consisted of four forms of presentation, the written forms of T_1 - self-instructional material and reading exercise and the more action dominated and less verbal (dialogue based) forms of T_2 – mono-acting, dramatized- multimedia (video recorded with movie strips show). Since the latter contained oral communication – though indirectly through dialogue - no oral form T_1 was included in T_3 verbal communication was limited to written forms. Thus T_3 combined direct verbal communication with indirect conveyance of cognitive messages and direct affective appeal of some dramatized-multimedia.

3.9 DEVELOPMENT OF MATERIALS AND PLANS

Each of the attitudes presented a total theme for the presentation. But it had to be analyzed into its different aspects, ideas of message, supportive facts and arguments, relationships and interpretation, implication and consequences etc., further a variety of situations in which they could be observable or they could be presented had to be identified, visualized and formulated in their details and sequences. From these had to be identified and delineated content suitable for talks, multidimensional and controversial issues suitable for panel discussion, information and logical arguments suitable for oral or written presentation, ideas and situations suitable for visual presentation (pictures, charts, etc.) were identified, situations suitable for development into stories (including those for film strips) with content and characters, events and movements, structure and plot, action, inferences and message, entertainment and education had also to be identified or imagined thought out in detail. All this demanded a lot of study, thinking and imagination. Discussion with a number of good teachers, writers, artists and other people knowledgeable in the content of the themes and the art and craft of such presentation helped to build up a wealth of ideas, which were sorted out and selected for the different presentations. While the essential content and message of the different treatments had to be the same in the case of each attitude the details, the situations and the techniques and forms of representation had to vary with the forms of presentation.

The script for reading passages, self-instructional materials, story telling, and film strips were prepared with the help of a number of good teachers (including language teachers) technical people and other writers. It was ensured that the attitude scale items were not included in the text of any presentation.

In the preparation of dramatized-multimedia communication for film strips expert guidance was taken from students of Theatre Arts, Department of Theatre Arts, Andhra University, the staff of All India Radio (Prasar Bharathi), Doordarshan and Local TV channels (City Cable), Vizag film society, Visakhapatnam in an attempt to present only that much content which could be easily communicated within the stipulated time in a very effective manner.

Then the help of more experienced teachers was sought in scrutinizing the scripts and in preparing charts. For selection and preparation of charts on casteism guidance was sought from the staff of District Social Welfare Office and District Public Relation Office and staff of Visakhapatnam, which sends teams to various schools and colleges and organizes its own presentations.

In the preparation of materials for casteism, help was obtained from the staff of Social Welfare Ministry, Government of Andhra Pradesh, as they are also involved in similar presentations. Recorded film strips of CD on **"manual work, casteism and family planning'** were prepared with the help of the Rajesh digital studio, Visakhapatnam. Their CD players and technical person were taken from school to school (to all the five schools involved) at the pre-planned timings.

Treatment plans and materials were worked out, in all details well in advance, discussed, scrutinized thoroughly, and refined to the extent possible. Each of the treatments in respect of attitude was planned to have four one hour sessions. However, the schools generally have 45 minutes in their regular time-table, appreciating the purpose and potential value of the program; they readily agreed to make adjustment to provide one hour sessions. Regrouping of students was also formation of the required necessary for each session. Formation of the required experimental groups, arranging the communication aids required, a brief informal talk with the group at the beginning and a suitable interaction and conclusion as summing up at the end of the session, briefly laying stress on the salient points covered during the session would take some time, leaving 40 to 45 minutes, in each session for the 'activities-proper'. Details regarding tile time schedule content out lines and aids used (audio and video) for each session and for each treatment are given in Appendix B.

3.10 DESIGN OF THE EXPERIMENT

A pooled experimental design with two equivalents experimental groups from each of the schools was adopted for the study, to make the sample widely representative. A 3 × 3, rotation design with pre-test, post-test1 and post-test2 was followed in each school. There were three treatments to be tried out and there were two experimental groups in each school. The study was taken up for attitude. For the first groups in each school were allotted to the treatments by lots. Then the treatments in respect of the other attitudes were rotated cyclically as shown below:

Table 3.2 : Experimental groups

Attitude to	Experimental group		
	Group –I	Group –II	Group-III
Manual work	T_1	T_2	T_3
Casteism	T_2	T_3	T_1
Family planning	T_3	T_1	T_2

T_1 - Verbal-visual communication strategy

T_2 - Dramatized-multimedia communication strategy

T_3 - Integrated communication strategy of (T_1 and T_2)

In this design, there was no control group, it was not considered necessary as no significant change could be expected to occur in the attitudes (which are stable dispositions) in the span of ten days, without some special program or effort to produce such changes, as there is no question of retentivity for a control group in which the attitude change is not excepted to takes place, so for the two groups pre-test was administered. Then each group was given the chosen treatment. At the end of the treatment, the post-test was administered. At the ends of the treatment for the different groups were given a different treatment by rotation and the same kind of pre-test, post-test1 and post-test2 administration was done. Rotation was again applied when the third attitude was taken up, again with the pre-test and post-test employing the attitude scale concerned.

3.10.1. Sampling Procedure

The effective sample for the experimental study consisted of 600, IX standard students drawn from five schools in the of Visakhapatnam district. Initially 600 students (40 in each sub-group) were included and sought to be covered, but due to the absence of some of them either for number of only 30 students with full participation could be considered from each group, for the compilation of data. Even a sample of this size meant a total of $3 \times 30 \times 5 \times 3 = 1350$ subjects for the whole experiment which covered the attitudes.

Five schools in Visakhapatnam District, were chosen after careful consideration of their geographical location and composition of sex and SES of the students, so that more or less equal representation taken of all the subgroups under consideration. Overall, the sample could be taken as adequately representing the secondary school population of the district.

Out of five schools two schools were selected from rural revenue division in which one comes under Yelamanchili revenue division and the other in Narsipatnam revenue division. The other three school were selected in the Visakhapatnam urban revenue division, more specifically in and around greater Visakhapatnam.

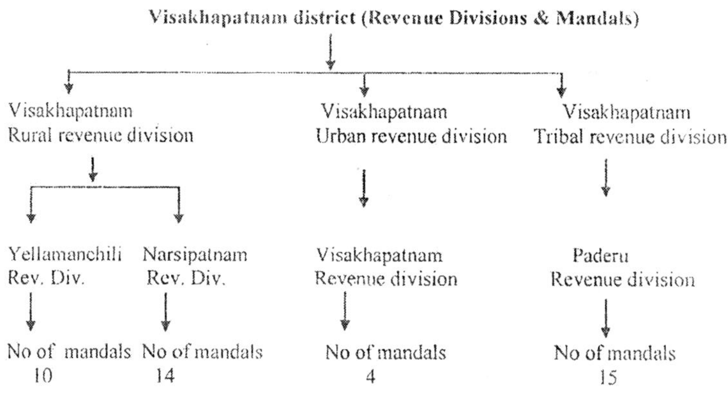

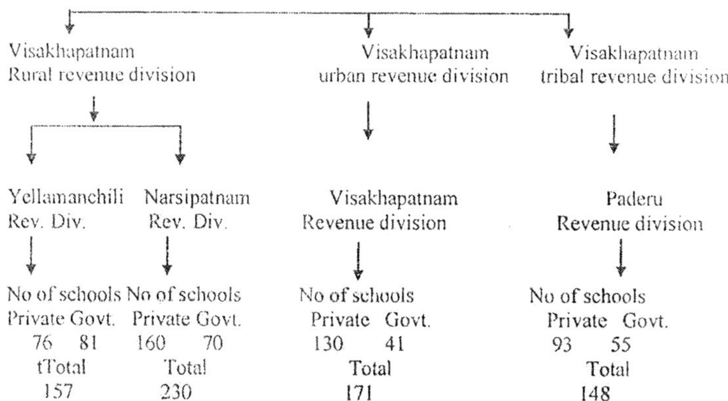

Table 3.3: Total population of IX class students in Visakhapatnam district during the academic year 2007-2008

Area	Boys	Girls	Total
Tribal	6820	5700	12520
Urban	7170	69290	13460
Rural	15929	13269	29198
Grand Total	**29919**	**25259**	**55178**

Table 3.4 : Sample distribution of student's school and locality wise strength

Sno	Name of the school	Location	No of sections Taken	No of students Taken per section	Total
1	M.V.D.M. High school	Visakhapatnam urban	3	40	120
2	K.D.P.M High School	Visakhapatnam urban	3	40	120
3	M.C.H.School, R.P.Peta, Urban	Visakhapatnam urban	3	40	120
4	APSWR School, Tallapalem	Visakhapatnam rural	3	40	120
5	APSWR School, Sabbavaram	Visakhapatnam rural	3	40	120

The schools had 3 sections of standard IX. Each school was persuaded to allot two sections at random, giving a total strength of over 120. Three experimental groups were formed by systematic sampling, including every third name in the attendance registers in one group. For example the students with roll numbers 1, 2, 3... In their school attendance register were grouped as shown below:

Table 3.5: Sampling procedure

Roll No of the student	Treatment group		
	Group-I	**Group-II**	**Group-III**
	1,4,7,10,13,16,19...	2,5,8,11,14,16...	3,6,9,12,15,18,21...

Thus, the sample was drawn with all the relevant considerations and precautions, to make it satisfactorily representative. The distribution of initial scores, in respect of each attitude under consideration was checked for normality to establish the representativeness of the sample. The values of mean, median, standard deviation, skewness and kurtosis are given.

Table 3.6: Descriptive statistics of the distribution of initial scores

Attitude	Mean	Median	Standard divination	Skewness	Kurtosis
Manual work	102.80	102.02	13.68	-0.03	0.24
Casteism	101.88	100.83	11.92	-0.11	0.22
Family planning	92.06	96.16	15.72	+0.38	0.25

Judged by the difference between mean and median and the values of skewness and kurtosis, the distribution could be taken as quite close to normal and so the sample could be taken as reasonably representative of a normal population.

3.10.2 Organisation of the experiment

At first the investigator had a detailed discussion with the relevant specialists, heads of institutions and the teachers concerned (of standard IX in the selected schools) and built up a clear understanding of the objectives, procedures and organizational requirements of the whole program from pre-test administration, through grouping and experimental treatment to post-test1 and post-test2 in the case of attitude. It was decided to have 4 sessions for each treatment over a period of two weeks or 10 days, so it was planned that in a period of 15 days all the experimental groups, in the five schools, would have pre-test, four sessions of the treatment concerned and the post-test1 at the end of the treatment. After a gap of six months the post-test2 is conducted and taking into consideration the location of the schools. The working hours of schools that worked on shift-system, etc.., a comprehensive program (schedule) was prepared well-in-advance and was distributed to all the heads of the institutions for each of the attitudes and it was ensured that no school would have more than a session a day about 45 days Thus, the whole experimental program took the subjects in each school formed themselves into groups as planned and previously notified, at the beginning of each session. The groups met in halls/rooms, away from each other for practical convenience, at any time there were only two sessions in progress at a school; This was achieved by suitably by combining T_3 (Integrated group) with either T_1 or T_2 according to the activities scheduled. For example T_3, group was combined with T_1 group when self-instructional material was administered or reading exercise was organized. Similarly the students assigned to T_3 group sat along with T_2 group when dramatized-multimedia communication (film strips show) in progress. There was no proper of accommodation: nor was the combining of groups detrimental to the effective-ness of the experiment because the students were used to large class teaching; further large groups did not matter in treatments like individualized learning/reading activities.

The experimenter sought the help of local class teachers to maintain discipline in the experimental groups and out- side the halls (from disturbances by others) and in organizational matters. They also took responsibility for the administration of pre-tests under the guidance and super vision of the investigator. Pre-test in each case was given to all subjects in the school at the same times too the post-test-1 and post-test-2. Each test was completed in all the schools in a day or two. For administration of tests detailed instructions were given first, response making illustrated on the blackboard and clarifications given when doubts were raised before the subjects were asked to respond to the items in the scale; this was very smooth after the first administration session, as they developed familiarity with the process. The data on SES was collected on a personal data bank at the end of the last testing session.

3.11 LIMITATIONS OF THE STUDY

The study was subject to the following limitations:

I. The study was limited to secondary school pupils of Visakhapatnam district, with 600 pupils of IX standard from five schools (five co-education schools located in different parts of the distract) to represent the population fairly adequately (However, the effective sample with complete attendance and data was only 495).

II. As groups had to be taken from schools (with in their organizational schedule) intact class groups were taken for practical convenience, in organizing the large number of sessions as mentioned, number of sessions as mentioned above. So the sample was not that strictly randomized, but the sub-groups for different treatments were chosen systematically. All care was taken to make them satisfactorily representative of the secondary school population in the city and of different strata by sex and SES by taking one schools and occupational communities. Thus, perfect stratification or randomization was not feasible but systematic sampling was done with intact groups in each school to from the two experimental groups. In any case, a donation design was adopted for the two groups for the one treatment vis-a-vis attitudes in school.

III. Learner participation was not provided for, as it was not feasible to train pupils from different schools for activities like skits, play-lets and story telling. But presentation by the same team, specially selected and trained for the purpose, helped to control the communicator variable (comparable to teacher in instruction).

IV. The experimental treatment for changing each attitude was limited to four sessions within a span of 30 days - as even this would demand 5 × 3 × 3 × 4 =180 sessions.

V. The pre-test, treatment and post-test1 followed a gap of six months in fairly quick succession in respect of each attitude - to suit the convenience of the schools. Retention effects were studied - after a six months lapse of time, by conducting post test-2 to assess if the changes achieved were transient or genuine/stable.

VI. Including only items that discriminated between top and the bottom groups at 0.01 level of significance, ensuring reasonably high internal consistency and overall discrimination validated the attitude scales. It was not possible to check discrimination between nominated groups or the correlation with another accepted tool (which did not exist) in order to validate the whole scale.

VII. After a careful study of the longitudinal studies cited in chapter II, it is fact that an optimum period of six months will serve as an ideal gap for this study, Peterson et al. (1988) and Anders, C. and Berg, R. (2005).

3.12 Analysis of data

3.12.1 Scoring

The initial scores in respect of each subject were obtained, by scoring the pre-test forms and the final scores, a respect of the same students by scoring the post-test1 and Post-test2 forms. Scoring keys were prepared and scoring was done by placing the key along side the marked responses. Suitable weightage, as prescribed (5, 4, 3, 2, 1 and 1, 2, 3,4, 5 for the positive and negative items respectively) was given. The sum of weighted scores was taken as the total score on each scale. Thus, in respect of each student, both the initial and final scores, the attitude scales, were obtained.

If, by chance, any item was not rated by a subject, it vas assumed that his choice would be 'C' which stood or 'undecided' and the scoring was done accordingly. The data obtained in regard to sea was scored in accordance with the instruction and formula of weights given by scale Prof. R.A. Singh and Prof. S.K. Saxena and the subjects were classified as high (H), middle (M) low (L) and very low (VL) stratum.

3.12.2 Tabulation of data

The scores obtained by each student on pre-test and post-test1and post-test2 (initial, test1 and test2 final scores) on the attitude, scale-wise, treatment-wise, school-wise and the gain score (difference between the final and initial scores) calculated and recorded for each attitude; data on clarification by sex (boys, girls) and by SES (high (H), middle (M) and low (L)) were also added. These made up the total set of data collected in the study and require testing the three major hypotheses set forth.

3.13. STATISTICAL TECHNIQUES USED IN ANALYZING AND INTERPRETING THE DATA

Statistics is the body of mathematical techniques or processes for gathering, describing, organizing and interpreting numerical data. Since, research often yields such quantitative data; statistics is basic tool of measurement and research. The research worker who uses statistics is concerned with more than the manipulation of data, statistical methods goes back to fundamental purposes of analysis. Research in education may deal with two types of statistical analysis of data.

1. Descriptive statistical analysis
2. Inferential statistical analysis

In this study, the investigation have been carried out by the descriptive statistical analysis such as calculating measures of central tendency like mean and calculating measures of dispersion like standard deviation. For testing the null hypothesis (Significance of the difference between means) the **t-test** and **analysis of variance (ANOVA)** have been used by the investigator. To find out the paired mean difference and the level of significance Scheffe's Post Hoc test was administrated with the help of SPSS package.

3.14. SUMMARY

Based on item analysis of the scores obtained in the pre-test, post-test 1, post test 2 of three attitudes, "manual work, casteism and family planning" using VISAM, VISAC, VISAF scales respectively all the test items the attitude scales mentioned above have item validity. All are significant at 0.01 level. The obtained scores of attitude scales pre– test, post–test1 and post-test2 of three attitudes were collected to study difference between the mean development of attitude of pre–test, post–test1 and post-test2 of standard IX students with in five schools which are three are in rural area and two are in urban area in Visakhapatnam District, State of Andhra Pradesh, India using mean values, standard deviation, t- test and f- test (ANOVA).

CHAPTER 4

ANALYSIS AND INTERPRETATION OF DATA

4.0. Introduction

The analysis and interpretation of data represents the application of deductive and inductive logic to the research process. The data is often classified by division into subgroups and are then analyzed and synthesized in such a way that hypothesis may be accepted or rejected. The end result may be a new principle or generalization.

Analysis of data means studying the tabulated material in order to determine inherent facts or meanings. It involves bringing the down the existing complex factors into simpler parts and putting the parts together in new arrangements for the purpose of interpretation.

The study was indented to assess the significance of certain attitudinal change achieved through the three communication strategies, separately and in comparison. In addition, it was also sought to estimate the significance of relationship between sex, SES, caste, religion, parental qualification and the demographic sub-groups on the one hand and the original attitudes and the attitude changes achieved through the treatments on the other and also to test their retention after a gap of six months. Three main hypotheses on these had been formulated for verification in this regard (vide chapter – III, supra, 3.2).

Statistical analysis of data

Statistics is the body of mathematical techniques or processes for gathering, describing, organizing and interpreting numerical data. Since, research often yields such quantitative data; statistics is basic tool of measurement and research. The research worker who uses statistics is concerned with more than the manipulation of data, statistical methods goes back to fundamental purposes of analysis (vide chapter – III, supra 3.13).

Table 4.1: Scheeffe's Post Hoc Test (pre-test)

The gains in different strategies T_1,T_2, T_3 and the initial levels of attitudes (pre-test) towards VISAM, VISAC,VISAF scales

Teaching Strategy	VISAM			VISAC			VISAF		
	Mean Gains	F	Sig.	Mean Gains	F	Sig.	Mean Gains	F	Sig.
T_1	85.66			79.84			84.93		
T_2	86.25	0.10	0.91	80.14	0.86	0.96	84.98	0.16	0.86
T_3	86.04			79.88			85.61		

Fig. 4.1: Graph showing the mean gains of students in different attitudes

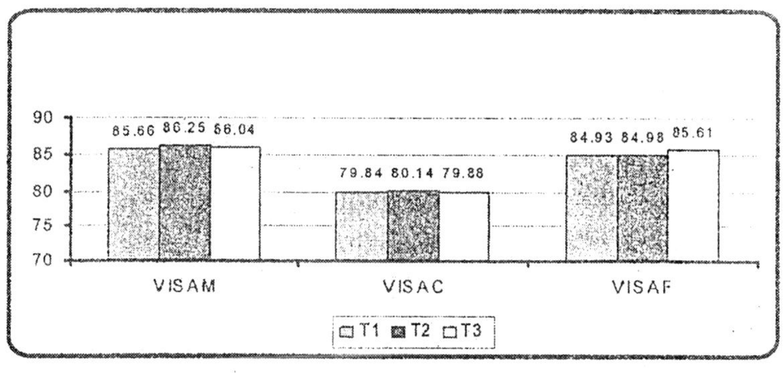

The table 4.1 indicates that the obtained F-ratio values of 0.10,0. 86, 0.16 among the three attitudes selected for the study in their pre-test are not significant. This reveals that there is no significant difference between these three groups of students based on their initial attitude towards manual work, casteism, family planning before teaching in different teaching strategies for selected for the research study. This indicates that the categorization of students into identical groups according to their characteristics has been systematically done.

4.1. CHANGE ACHIEVED IN THE ATTITUDE

4.1.1. Testing of hypothesis – I (i)

Table 4.2: Scheeffe's Post Hoc Test(pre-test & post-test1)

Mean gains between pre-test and post-test1 and 'F' ratios in respect of the three strategies (T_1, T_2, T_3) and the attitudes towards VISAM,VISAC,VISAF

Teaching Strategy	VISAM		VISAC		VISAF	
	Mean Gains	F	Mean Gains	F	Mean Gains	F
T_1	6.88	417.33**	9.14	210.82**	5.33	121.03**
T_2	16.83	508.45**	19.17	360.29**	15.87	100.22**
T_3	11.22	581.95**	15.30	343.07**	12.62	194.57**

Fig. 4.2

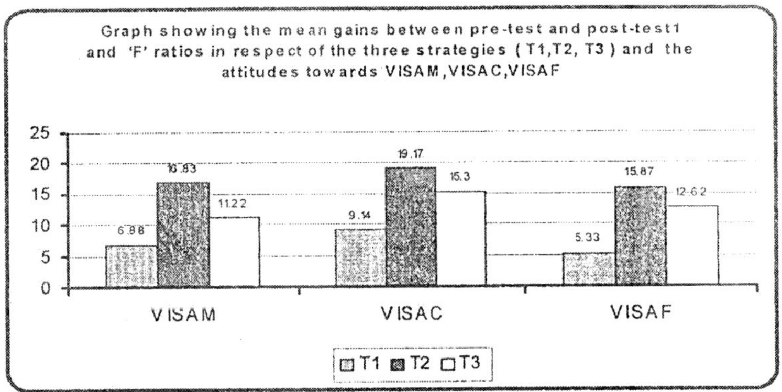

Table 4.2 presents the first major hypothesis-I (i) on the effect of the three communication strategies verbal-visual, dramatized -multimedia and Integrated in the changing the attitude to manual work, casteism, family planning had predicted that each of the three educational treatments as above would produce significant change in the desired direction in respect of the attitude concerned. It had also been decided that this hypothesis would be tested by the 'F' (ANOVA) test of significance of differences in means between pre-test and post-test1 scores on the attitude scale concerned. Hence the first part of H-I (i) is accepted and this is in line with the findings of this study are, in a way, consistent with those of Bennet (1955) that discussion technique produced significant attitude change, the finding of Eagly and Chalken (1975) that written modality was effective in conveying information - hence quite persuasive, and also with those of Williams (1975), Bradac, Konsky and Davies (1976) that live or video-taped messages induced greater attitude change than audio-taped messages, Rao PS (1984).

The second part of the H-I (ii) is tested by ANOVA Scheeffe's post Hoc test Mean gains between post-test1 and post-test2 and 'F' ratios in respect of the three strategies (T_1,T_2,T_3) and the attitudes towards VISAM,VISAC,VISAF with the help of SPSS package, would be used in verifying the hypothesis, vide Table 4.3.

The major steps in the calculation of F-ratio in the case of the three attitudes are shown in Tables 4.2. All the F-ratios were found significant. This implied that there were significant differences between the three treatments in respect of the effect produced in terms of gains or changes the attitude. Which means that T_2,T_3,T_1 are persuasive in that order for

VISAM and VISAC Scales, where as T_3,T_2 and T_1 are persuasive in that order.

The analysis of the results in section –IV, supra 4.3 revealed that T_1,T_2 and T_3 were all quite effective in producing changes in the attitude. The ANOVA- Scheffe's Post Hoc test was administrated with the help of SPSS package: result showed that there was significant difference among the three treatments in respect of their effects. Combining the two analyses, in respect of VISAM and VISAF scales we can conclude that while all the treatments seemed to be quote productive and promising, the treatment Dramatized–multimedia (filmstrips show) prepared by the investigator made for the wider change than the other, also the prestige suggestion "might" also have played a part in this. Where as in the VISAF scale, the T_3 sesames to be more powerful in producing a more significant attitude change than the other. These conclusions go along with the studies of as suggested by the studies of Aronson (1966); Hovland, Janis and Kelly (1952) and Aronson and Golden (1962), Rao, P.S (1984), Vellei Swamy, M. (2007). However, with the difference in treatments, there inevitably would come differences in the details of content, structure and features of presentation apart from differences in the types of activities as intended (though the essence of the message was intended to be the same), the ultimate effect would possible depend more on the cognitive and affective content of the communication and its source, clarity, structure and forcefulness than on the mere for mode of communication.

4.1.2. Testing of hypothesis – I (ii)

Table 4.3: Scheeffe's post Hoc test values of different groups

T_1,T_2 and T_3 strategies and retentive of the attitudes change (Post-test1 and post-test2)

Teaching Strategy	VISAM		VISAC		VISAF	
	Mean Gains	P	Mean Gains	P	Mean Gains	P
T_1	21.07	0.00**	23.51	0.00**	19.76	0.00**
T_2	23 20	0 00**	31.99	0.00**	13.87	0 00**
T_3	24.53	0.00**	29.43	0.00**	25.33	0.00**

Fig. 4.3

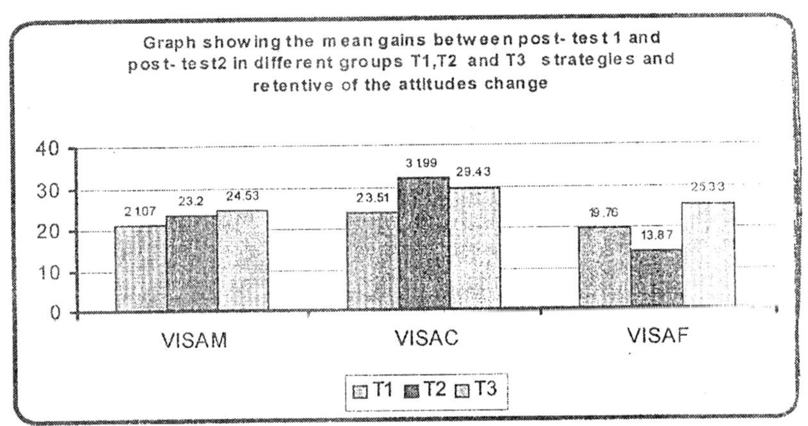

The second part of the H-I (ii) is tested by ANOVA Scheeffe's post Hoc test mean gains between post-test1 and post-test2 and 'F' ratios in respect of the three strategies (T_1,T_2,T_3) and the attitudes towards VISAM,VISAC,VISAF with the help of SPSS package, would be used in verifying the hypothesis.

Going by the values of Table 4.3, all the 'p' values are significant at 1% level, indicating that the attitude change produced was very much retained after a period of six months. So we can safely conclude that that the attitude change produced by T_1,T_2,T_3 is retained after six months. Hence H-I (ii) is accepted.

Also it is observed that T_3,T_2,T_1 for VISAM, T_2,T_3,T_1 for VISAC and T_3,T_1,T_2 for VISAF, in that order retained the induced change. This conclusion support the studies of Etaugh et al. (1982), Peterson et al. (1988)· Anders, C. and Berg, R. (2005), Courter et al. (2007) and oppose the study of Alison Kelly. (1986), McKinnan et al. (2000) and Twist. L. et al. (2004).

4.2 TESTING OF HYPOTHESIS: H-II

4.2.1. Comparative effects of the three treatments

The second major hypothesis of the study was that there would be no significant difference among the treatments in respect of the attitude changed produced. It is also proposed in the earlier chapter that the technique of ANOVA - Scheffe's Post Hoc test was administrated with the help of SPSS package, would be used in verifying the hypothesis.

The 'F' values of table 4.2 indicate that the all treatments were quite effective in producing highly significant attitude change in the desired direction. But they differ significantly in producing the same. So this part of hypothesis H-II(i) is rejected.

Going by the 'F' values (Table 4.2) and mean gains between pre-test and post-test1 scores, and the strategy T_1 (verbal-visual communi-cation) appears to be the weakest of the three strategies – in producing the desired attitude change in the students. This might be so because T_1 is very similar to the routine teaching – learning process followed by the schools and hence could not evoke sufficient interest from them. But the T_1 treatment seems to be of some interest to students of the castiesm group and it falls in line with their perception of the castesim.

Fig. 4.4

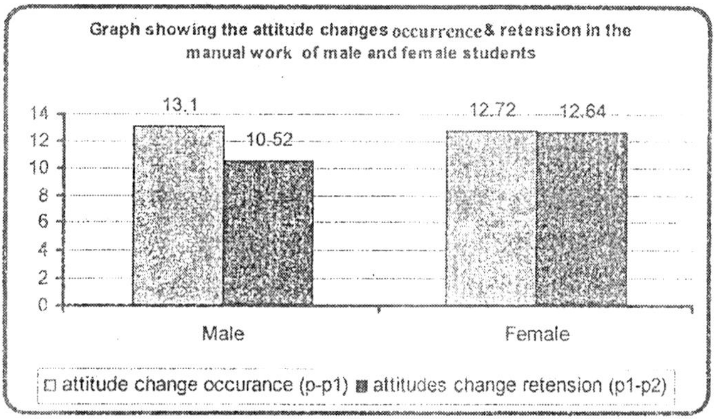

Graph showing the attitude changes occurrence& retension in the manual work of male and female students

13.1
10.52
12.72
12.64
14
12
10
8
6
4
2
0
Male
Female
□ attitude change occurance (p-p1) ■ attitudes change retension (p1-p2)

Coming to T_2 it produced significant changes in the desired direction in respect of the three attitudes, while the dramatized-multimedia strategy (T_2) was highly productive of change, the case of attitude to casteism. The only possible interpre-tation seemes to be that the clear and direct appeal of the messages conveyed verbally in T_1 and T_3, made an impact on the cognitive structures and feelings concerned and multimedia under T_3 strengthened the effect of the appeal, but multimedia by itself would be more powerful, with its direct affective appeal, if the film strips and the theme had strong multimedia content to wards casteism.

As for as T_3 is concerned, it could produce the best attitude change in the case of VISAC, as T_1 did and the same criteria might have been same as discussed earlier the messages delivered through different forms of visual-verbal communication could be made fairly well elucidated, elaborated, articulated, repeated in different forms and contexts, adequately integrated and properly emphasized in terms of the essence or conclusions,

Fig. 4.5

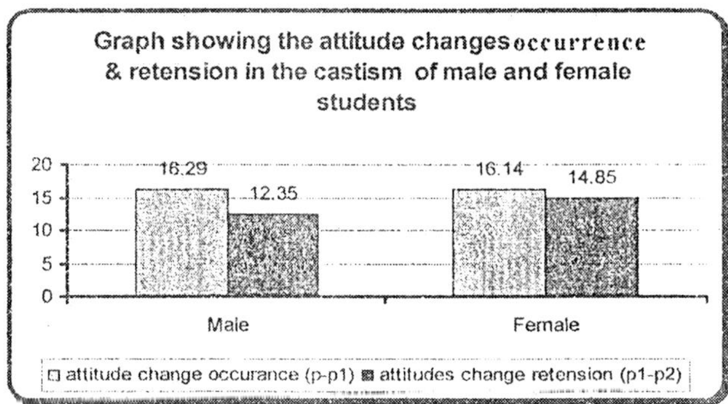

Fig. 4.6

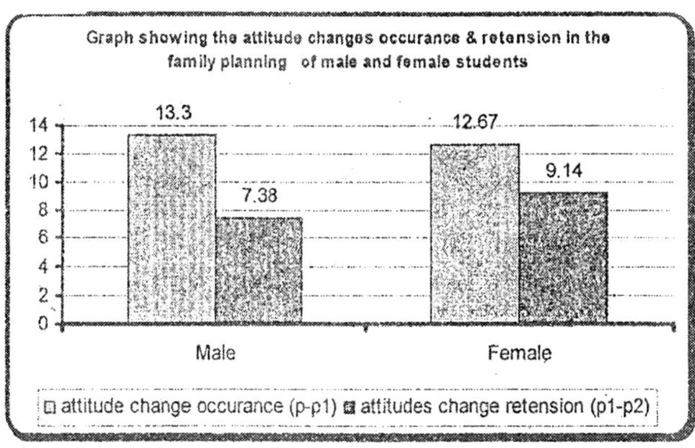

and students who are used to such treatments in regular instruction would be able to receive, register and process such information fairly effectively. This would necessarily produce a clear change. The messages conveyed through dramatized and multimedia (film strips) activities might often be qualified as of the 'high interference type', but it could still be more clear and strong; further the interesting dramatized and multimedia features interesting the story, the situations, the events, the characterization, the action and movements, and the gestures and expressions with their direct affective appeal and entertainment value- apart from the creation of a mood favorable for reception - could make for a deeper impression and internalization, if the medium is handled with intelligence and imagination, exploiting its potential.

The findings of this study are, in a way, consistent with those of Bennet (1955) that dis-cussion technique produced significant attitude change, the finding of Eagly and Chalken (1975) that written modality was effective in conveying information - hence quite persuasive, and also with those of Williams (1975), Bradac, Konsky and Davies (1976) that live or video-taped messages induced greater attitude change than audio-taped messages, Rao, P.S (1984).

Testing the second part of the major hypothesis H-II(ii) from the above table 4.3, all the 'p' values are significant at 0.01 level. So we reject the null hypothesis formulated, so we can safely conclude that that the attitude change produced by T_1,T_2,T_3 is retained after six months. Hence H-II (ii) is rejected.

Also it is observed that T_3,T_2,T_1 for VISAM, T_2,T_3,T_1 for VISAC and T_3,T_1,T_2 for VISAF in that order retained the induced change. This conclusion support the studies of Etaugh et al. (1982), Peterson et al. (1988), Anders, C. and Berg, R. (2005), Courter et al. (2007) and opposes the study by Alison Kelly (1986), Mckinnan et al. (2000) and Twist. L. et al. (2004).

4.3 TESTING OF HYPOTHESIS: H-III

4.3.1 Testing of hypothesis: H-III (i)

Table 4.4: 't'-values for the differences between the means of the sex sub groups

Attitude	Attitude / Test	Sex	Mean	t-value
Manual Work	Attitudes changes occurrence (p-p1)	Male	13.10	0.74
		Female	12.72	
	Attitudes change Retention (p1-p2)	Male	10.52	1.61
		Female	12.64	
Casteism	Attitudes changes occurrence (p-p1)	Male	16.29	0.19
		Female	16.14	
	Attitudes change Retention (p1-p2)	Male	12.35	1.73
		Female	14.85	
Family Planning	Attitudes changes occurrence (p-p1)	Male	13.30	0.99
		Female	12.67	
	Attitudes change Retention (p1-p2)	Male	7.38	1.43
		Female	9.14	

From the Table 4.4 none of the "t" values was found to be significant. The null hypothesis therefore is sustained. There did not seem to be any significant difference between boys and girls, on the one hand, and positive changes produced in the attitude on the other. In other words, the treatments had more or less the same effect on children of the two sexes.

The findings of this study regarding sex and attitude change conform with those of Barber and Calverley (1964), Eagly (1976) and did not support those of Knower (1936), Weitzenhoffer (1959), Stukat (1958), King (1956), Janis and Field (1959), Ableson and Lesser (1959), London (1963) and Hilgard (1965), Croucher et al. (1982), Rao, P.S (1984), Crouter et al. (2007) and Oppose the study Janet et al. (1997).

As far as the retentivity of the attitude change thus produced, none of the 't' values is found to be significant, we can conclude that there is no significant difference in the retaining ability also.

4.3.2 Testing of hypothesis: H-III (ii)

Fig. 4.7

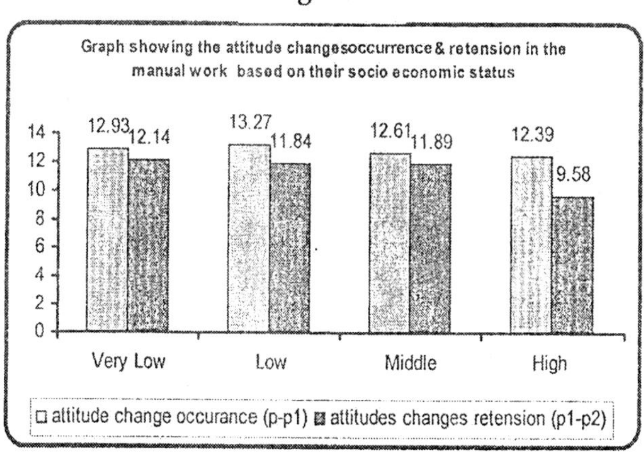

Table 4.5 : 'F' values for the differences between means of sub-groups socio economic status (SES)

Attitude	Attitude /Test	SES	Mean	F -value
Manual work	Attitudes changes occurrence (p-p1)	Very Low	12.93	0.60
		Low	13.27	
		Middle	12.61	
		High	12.39	
	Attitudes change retention (p1-p2)	Very Low	12.14	0.26
		Low	11.84	
		Middle	11.89	
		High	9.58	
Casteism	Attitudes changes occurrence (p-p1)	Very Low	14.07	0.34
		Low	16.22	
		Middle	16.32	
		High	16.21	
	Attitudes change retention (p1-p2)	Very Low	15.93	0.42
		Low	14.02	
		Middle	13.80	
		High	11.06	
Family planning	Attitudes changes occurrence (p-p1)	Very Low	12.64	0.87
		Low	13.48	
		Middle	12.43	
		High	13.36	
	Attitudes change retention (p1-p2)	Very Low	10.43	1.05
		Low	7.19	
		Middle	9.35	
		High	8.12	

Fig. 4.8

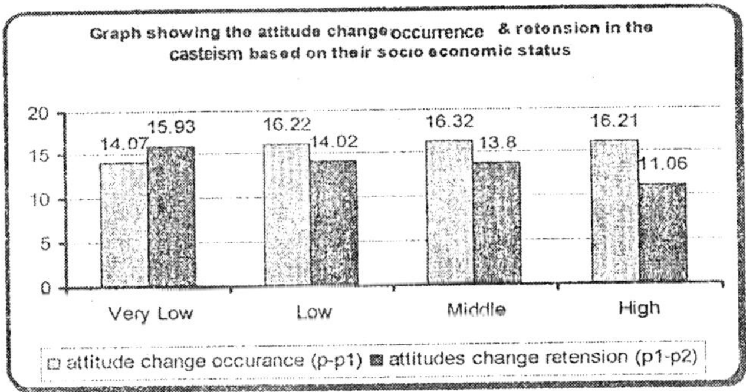
Graph showing the attitude change occurrence & retension in the casteism based on their socio economic status
20
15
10
5
0
14.07
15.93
16.22
14.02
16.32
13.8
16.21
11.06
Very Low
Low
Middle
High
attitude change occurance (p-p1)
attitudes change retension (p1-p2)

Fig. 4.9

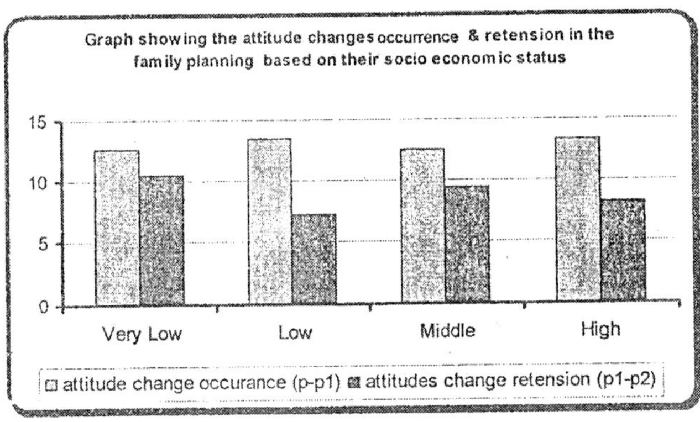
Graph showing the attitude changes occurrence & retension in the family planning based on their socio economic status
15
10
5
0
Very Low
Low
Middle
High
attitude change occurance (p-p1)
attitudes change retension (p1-p2)

Table 4.6, shows that the there is no significance between the demographic sub groups. Both the urban and rural groups reacted in the same was to the programme conducted regarding the three attitudes-except in the case casteism where the attitude change is pronounced in the urban groups and after a gap of six months also this is to be expected because of the urban influence on caste. As far as the retentivity is concerned none of 't' values is significant. So all the groups retained the attitude change obtained in even after six months.

Table 4.6: 't' values for the differences between means of sub-groups by Demographic area (Rural/Urban)

Attitude	Attitude/Test	Demographic Area	Mean	t-value
Manual work	Attitudes changes occurrence (p p1)	Urban	12.49	1.70
		Rural	13.37	
	Attitudes change retention (p1-p2)	Urban	11.39	0.56
		Rural	12.13	
Casteism	Attitudes changes occurrence (p-p1)	Urban	16.90	2.13*
		Rural	15.34	
	Attitudes change retention (p1-p2)	Urban	13.66	0.17
		Rural	13.91	
Family planning	Attitudes changes occurrence (p-p1)	Urban	12.58	1.27
		Rural	13.39	
	Attitudes change retention (p1-p2)	Urban	8.30	0.14
		Rural	8.48	

*Significant at 0.05 level in casteism of p-p1

Fig. 4.10

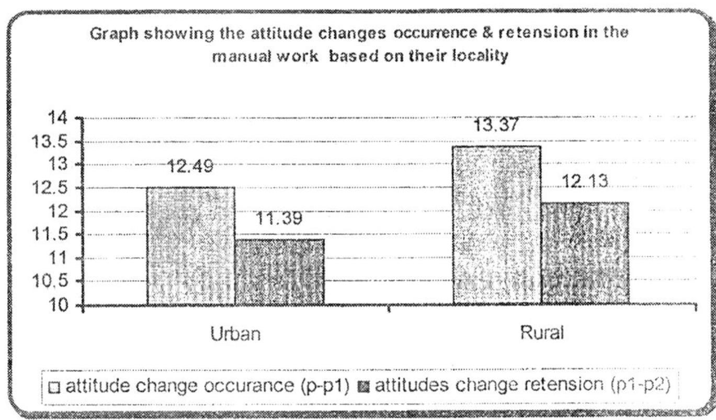

Fig. 4.11

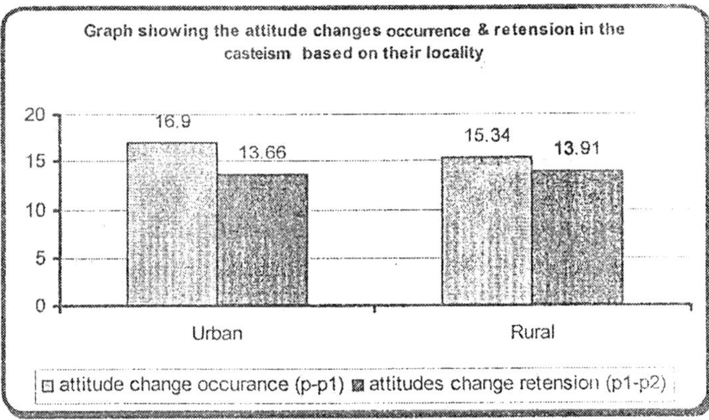

Fig. 4.12

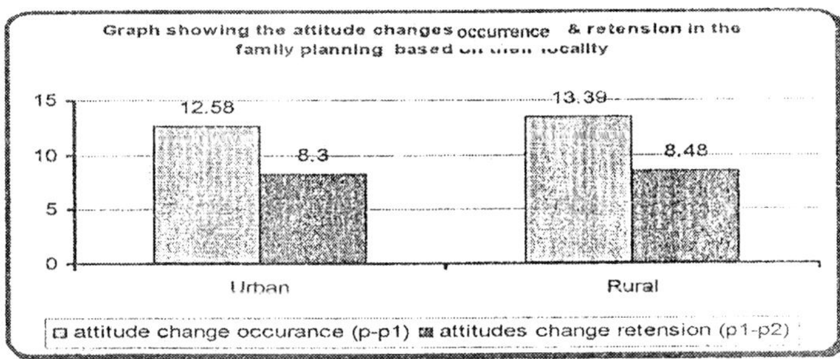

4.3.4 Testing of hypothesis: H III (iv)

Table 4.7: 'F' values for the differences between means of sub-groups by caste

Attitude	Attitude /Test	Caste	Mean	F -value
Manual Work	Attitudes changes occurrence (p-p1)	OC	12.34	2.60
		BC	13.14	
		SC	11.98	
		ST	16.08	
	Attitudes change retention (p1-p2)	OC	14.20	1.33
		BC	11.74	
		SC	9.77	
		ST	10.31	
Casteism	Attitudes changes occurrence (p-p1)	OC	15.46	0.57
		BC	16.23	
		SC	17.01	
		ST	15.31	
	Attitudes change retention (p1-p2)	OC	16.20	1.08
		BC	13.79	
		SC	11.83	
		ST	12.08	
Family planning	Attitudes changes occurrence (p-p1)	OC	12.97	1.22
		BC	13.20	
		SC	11.73	
		ST	14.46	
	Attitudes change retention (p1-p2)	OC	7.96	0.56
		BC	8.84	
		SC	7.78	
		ST	4.46	

Fig. 4.13

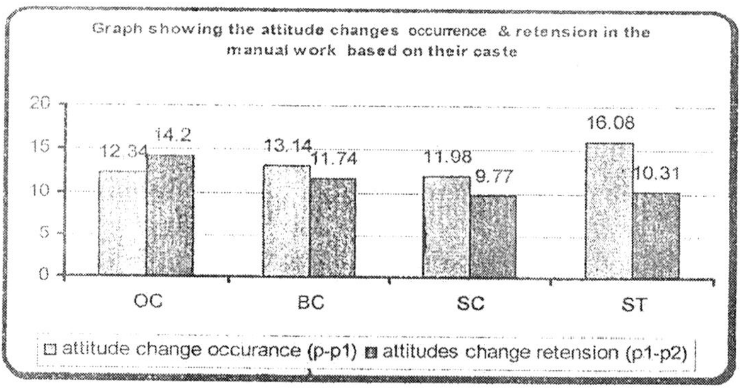

Fig. 4.14

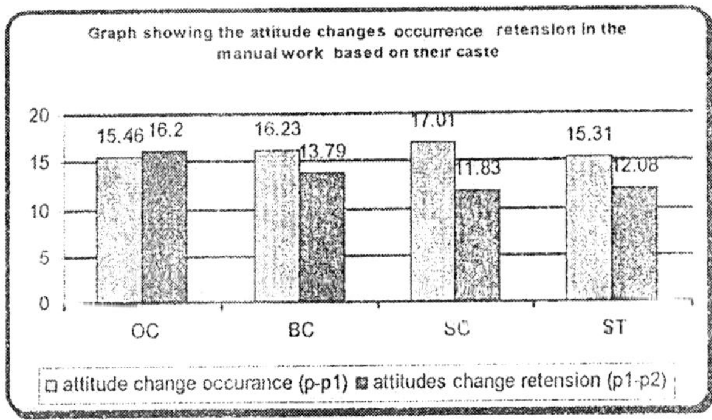

Fig. 4.15

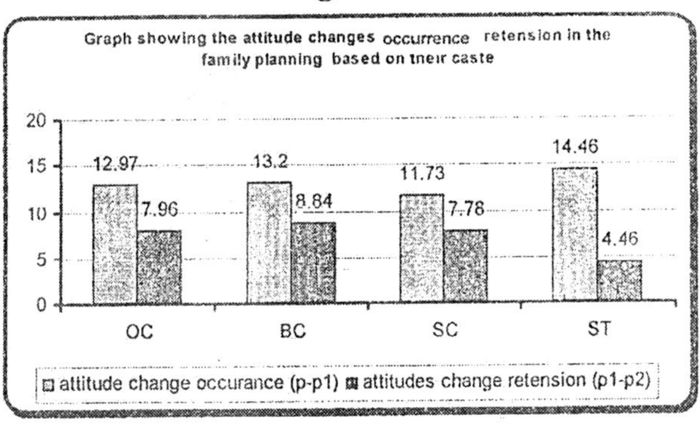

Table 4.7 shows that the 'F' values of the different caste sub groups were not significant. So all the sub groups accepted the programme and produced the attitude change in the desired direction. It clearly indicates there is no difference in the retention of the attitude change programme conducted.

Also found that the attitude change this indicated was retained by of all the subgroups.

4.3.5 Testing of hypothesis: H-III (v)

Table 4.8: 'F' values for the differences between means of sub-groups by religion

Attitude	Attitude/Test	Religion	Mean	F -value
Manual Work	Attitudes changes occurrence (p-p1)	Hindu	12.89	5.26**
		Muslim	15.12	
		Christian	12.26	
	Attitudes change retention (p1-p2)	Hindu	11.15	0.74
		Muslim	13.79	
		Christian	11.92	
Casteism	Attitudes changes occurrence (p-p1)	Hindu	15.89	5.38**
		Muslim	13.40	
		Christian	17.38	
	Attitudes change retention (p1-p2)	Hindu	13.25	0.70
		Muslim	16.13	
		Christian	13.82	
Family planning	Attitudes changes occurrence (p-p1)	Hindu	12.49	9.22**
		Muslim	16.85	
		Christian	12.48	
	Attitudes change retention (p1-p2)	Hindu	8.49	0.59
		Muslim	6.46	
		Christian	8.75	

** Significance at 0.01 level.

Fig. 4.16

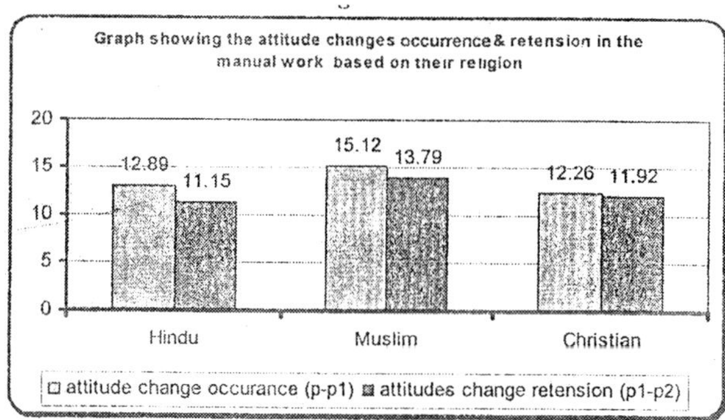

Fig. 4.17

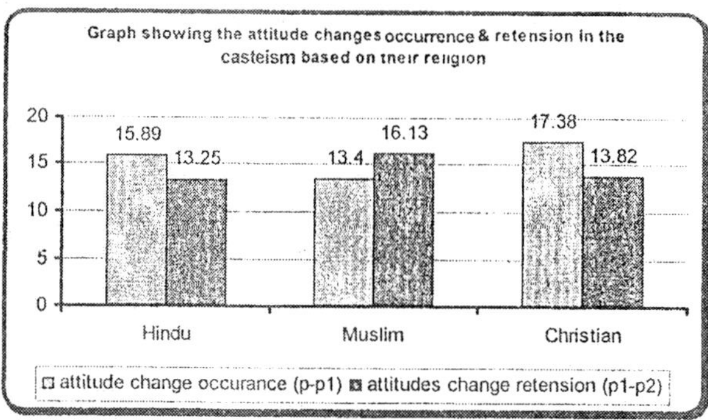

Fig. 4.18

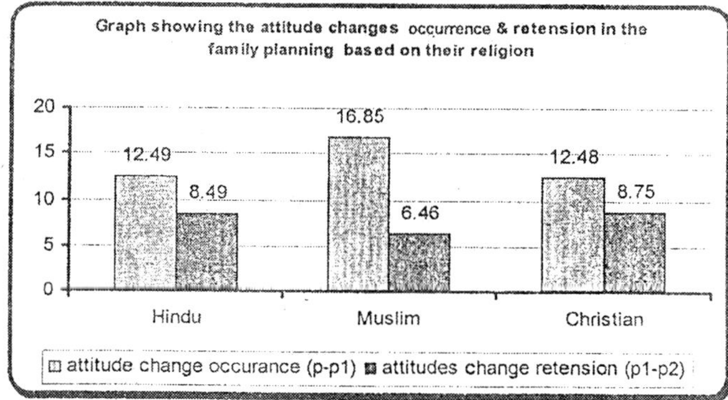

From the above Table 4.8 it is seen that all the 'F' ratios are significant in respect of the production of attitude change. Hence the null hypothesis H-III (v) is rejected. Going by the 'F' values of the Hindu, Muslim and Christian subgroups mainly the Muslim sub group showed the better tendency to be influenced by the programme as compared to the other two groups. Going by the demographic factors that influenced the Muslim sub groups, all those students are from the urban schools. This might have influenced their attitude towards manual work.

As far as the casteism is concerned, religious sub-groups are concerned, the Christian sub group reacted possibility to the programme of inducing the attitude change in the required direction rather sharply. This may be due to fact that the Christian students involved in the programme are converted types from the lower caste groups-like BC and SC.

In the programme that was intended to induce the attitude change towards family planning, the Muslim sub-groups were the most influenced and this showed a welcome sign for the future effective implementation of the family planning programmes in our state and country.

From the above Table 4.8, none of the differences the means of the religious sub groups were found significant and the null hypothesis is retained. We can conclude that all the religious sub groups retained the attitude change.

4.3.6 Testing of hypothesis: H-III (vi)

Table 4.9: 'F' values for the differences between means of sub-groups by parental educational qualification

Attitude	Attitude/Test	Parental qualification	Mean	F –value
Manual work	Attitudes changes occurrence (p-p1)	Primary	12.64	0.31
		Secondary	13.08	
		Higher	12.86	
	Attitudes change retention (p1-p2)	Primary	11.07	0.54
		Secondary	12.54	
		Higher	11.71	
Casteism	Attitudes changes occurrence (p-p1)	Primary	16.22	2.82
		Secondary	15.51	
		Higher	18.22	
	Attitudes change retention (p1-p2)	Primary	13.13	0.70
		Secondary	14.81	
		Higher	12.92	
Family planning	Attitudes changes occurrence (p-p1)	Primary	12.34	3.00
		Secondary	12.98	
		Higher	14.80	
	Attitudes change retention (p1-p2)	Primary	8.92	0.23
		Secondary	8.01	
		Higher	8.54	

Fig. 4.19

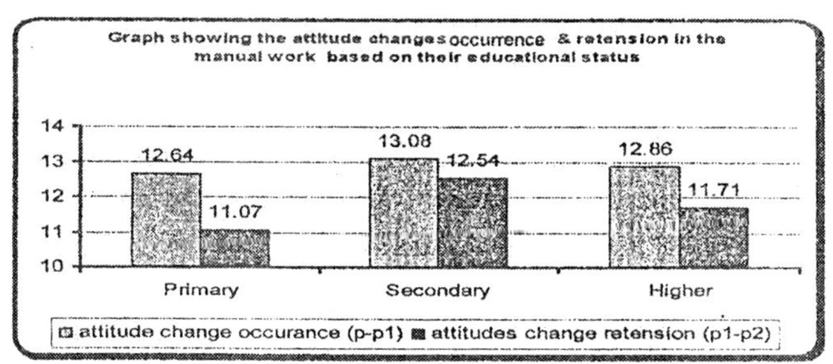

Fig. 4.20

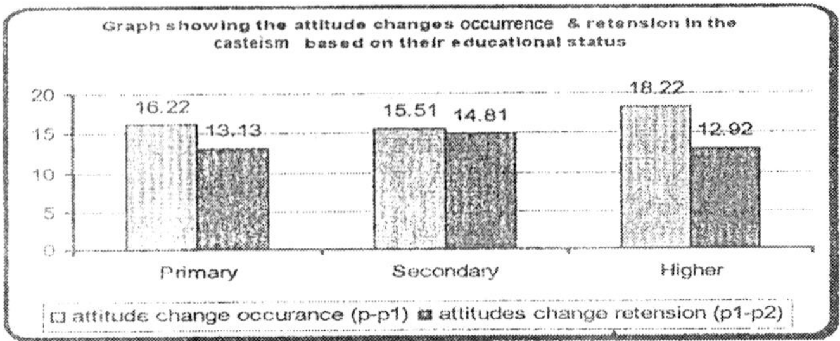

Fig. 4.21

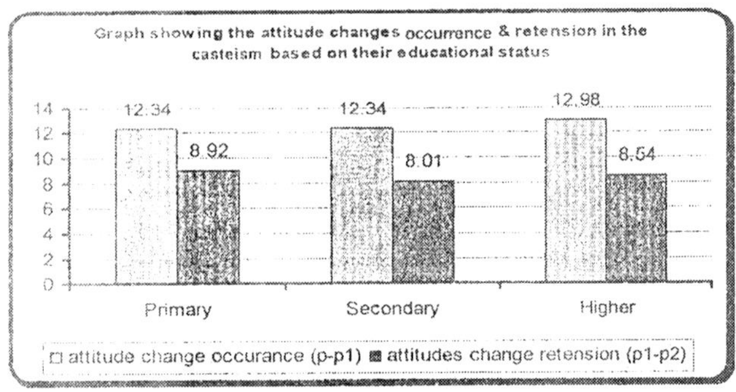

CHAPTER 5

SUMMARY, FINDINGS AND CONCLUSIONS

5.0 INTRODUCTION

Attitudes form not only colorful determinants of behavior but also an absorbing area of research. Formation or change of such attitudes, then, becomes the concern of the society in general, and on education in particular. In the present Indian context, attitudes in respect of family planning, casteism and manual work - among other things-seem to be of special importance. (Theories of attitude change, and a wide range of studies on attitudes, especially attitude change, have been reviewed).

5.1 OBJECTIVES OF THE STUDY

5.1.1 Effects of the three treatments in producing attitude change

All the means of differences between pre-test, post-test1 and post -test2 scores were positive (vide Table 4.2, Supra) indicating gains in the direction of more positive attitude, in respect of all the three treatments and the three attitudes. The differences indicating the quantum of changes or gain were statistically significant in all the nine cases at 0.01 levels. All the three treatments therefore proved to be quite productive and promising of marked changes in attitudes in the desired direction.

The findings of this study are in a way consistent with these of Bennet (1955) that discussion technique produced significant attitude change, the finding of Eagly and Chaiken (1975) that written modality was (superior) effective in conveying information –hence quite persuasive, and also with those of Williams (1975), Bradac, Konsky and Davies (1976) that live or video-taped messages induced greater attitude change than audio-taped messages, which in turn elicited greater change than written messages, though the comparisons were not exactly on the same lines. Possibly, the content and quality of the presentation would be more important than the form in producing attitude change.

Also the observed from Table 4.3 all the 'p' values are significant indicating the level of retentivity of the achieved attitude change.

5.2 HYPOTHESIS OF THE STUDY

5.2.1 Interpretation of the pre-test scores (Initial attitude change)

The obtained F-ratio values from the vide table 4.1 of 0.10, 0.86, 0.16 among the three attitudes selected for the study in their pre-test is not significant. This reveals that there is no significant difference between these three groups of students based on their initial attitude towards manual work, casteism, family planning before teaching in different teaching strategies for selected for the research study. This also indicates that the categorization of students into identical groups according to their characteristics has been systematically done.

5.2.2 Comparative study of the effects of the three techniques and their retentivity

The null hypothesis (H II (i)) on differences in the effects of the three treatments was tested by ANOVA, F ratios and their retentivity by the Scheeffe's post Hoc test vide table 4.2 and 4.3 supra.

All the 'F' ratios are found significant at the 0.01 level indicating the differential effect of the three strategies. Table 4.2 presents the first major hypothesis-I (i) on the effect of the three communication strategies verbal-visual, dramatized-multimedia and Integrated (T_1, T_2, T_3) in the changing attitude to manual work, casteism, family planning had predicted that each of the three educational treatments as above would produce significant change in the desired direction in respect of the attitude concerned. It had also been decided that this hypothesis would be tested by the 'F' test of significance of differences in means between pre-test and post-test1 scores on the attitude scale concerned. Hence the first part of H-I (i) is accepted and this is in line with the Eagly and Chalken (1975) that written modality was effective in conveying information - hence quite persuasive, and also with those of Williams (1975), Bradac, Konsky and Davies (1976) that live or video-taped messages induced greater attitude change than audio-taped messages, Rao, P.S (1984).

The second part of the H-I (ii) is tested by ANOVA Scheeffe's post Hoc test mean gains between post-test1 and post-test2 and 'F' ratios in respect of the three strategies (T_1, T_2, T_3) and the attitudes towards VISAM, VISAC, VISAF with the help of SPSS package, would be used in verifying the hypothesis, vide Table 4.3.

The major steps in the calculation of F-ratio in the case of the three attitudes are shown in Table 4.2. All the F-ratios were found significant. This implied that there were significant differences between the three treatments in respect of the effect produced in terms of gains or changes the attitude. Which means that T_2, T_3, T_1 are persuasive in that order for VISAM and VISAC Scales, where as T_3, T_2 and T_1 are persuasive in that order.

5.3 FINDINGS OF THE STUDY

The analysis of the results in section --IV, supra 4.3 revealed that T_1, T_2 and T_3 were all quite effective in producing changes in the entire attitude. The ANOVA- Scheffe's Post Hoc test was administrated with the help of SPSS package; result showed that there was significant difference among the three treatments in respect of their effects. Combining the two analyses, in respect of VISAM and VISAF scales we can conclude that while all the treatments seemed to be quite productive and promising, the treatment dramatized--multimedia (filmstrips show) prepared by the investigator made for the wider change than the other, also the prestige suggestion might have come in, where as in the VISAF scale, the T_3 sesames to be more powerful in producing a more significant attitude change than the other. These conclusions go along with the studies of as suggested by the studies of and Aronson Hovland (1966), Janis and King (1954) and Aronson and Golden (1962), Etaugh et al. (1982) Rao, P.S (1984), Anders, C. and Berg, C. (2005), Courter et al. (2007), Vellei Swamy, M. (2007) and oppose the study of Alison Kelly (1986), Mckinnan et al. (2000) and Twist. L. et al. (2004). However, with the difference in treatments, there inevitably would come differences in the details of content, structure and features of presentation apart from differences in the types of activities as intended (though the essence of the message was intended to be the same), the ultimate effect would possible depend more on the cognitive and affective content of the communication and its source, clarity, structure and forcefulness than on the mode of communication.

5.3.1 The effect of the treatments on the sub-groups - Sex

Since none of the "t" values (Table 4.4 supra) was found to be significant. The null hypothesis therefore is sustained. There did not seem to be any significant difference between boys and girls on the one hand, and positive changes produced in the attitude on the other. In other words, the treatments had more or less the same effect on children of the two sexes.

The findings of this study regarding sex and attitude change conform to those of Barber and Calverley (1964) and Eagly (1975) did not support those of Knower (1936), Weitzenhoffer (1953), Stukat (1958), King (1956), Janis and Field (1959), Ableson and Lesser (1959)[1], and Hilgard, (1965), Rao, P.S (1984).

As far as the retentivity of the attitude change thus produced, none of the 't' values is found to be significant, we can conclude that there is no significant difference in the retaining ability also.

5.3.2 The effect of the treatments on the sub-groups – SES

The effect of the treatments none of the 'F' values (Table 4.5) were found significant so we can conclude that all the SES group's respondent to the attitude change programme in the same way – as well as in their retention one consisting finding in this study is that the middle income groups, remained at the middle level of their changing attitudes and retention capabilities.

5.3.3 The effect of the treatments on the sub-groups – Demographic sub-groups (urban and rural)

The effect of the treatments on (Table 4.6) shows that the there is no significance between the demographic sub groups both the urban and rural groups reacted in the same way to the programme conducted regarding the three attitudes- except in the case casteism where the attitude change is pronounced in the urban groups. After a gap of six months also this is to be expected because of the urban influence on caste. As far as the retention is concerned none of 't' values is significant. So all the groups retained the attitude change obtained even after six months.

5.3.4 The effect of the treatments on the sub-groups – Caste sub-groups

The effect of the treatments shows that the (Table 4.7) 'F' values of the different caste sub groups were not significant in the any case. Indicating that there is no difference in the reception of the attitude change programme conducted and in their retentivity chrematistic, nor on their retention.

5.3.5 The effect of the treatments on the sub-groups–Religion sub-groups

The effects of the treatments from the above Table 4.8, it is seen that all the 'F' ratios are significant in respect of the production of attitude change. Hence the null hypothesis H-III (v) is rejected. By going to the Hindu, Muslim and Christian sub-groups mainly the Muslim sub group showed the better tendency be influenced by the programme compared to the other two groups. Going by the demographic factors that influenced the Muslim sub groups, all those students are from the urban schools. This might have influenced their attitude towards manual work.

As far as the casteism religious sub groups are concerned the Christian sub-group reacted possibility to the programme of inducing the attitude change in the required direction. We may conclude that all the Christian students involved in the programme are converted types from the lower caste groups-like BC and SC.

In the programme that was intended to induce the attitude change towards family planning, the Muslim sub-groups was the most influenced and this showed be a welcome sign for the future effective implementation of the family planning programmes in our state/country.

From the (Table 4.8) some of the differences the means of the religious sub groups were found significant and the null hypothesis is retained. We can conclude that all the religious sub-groups retained induced attitude changes.

5.3.6 The effect of the treatments on the sub-groups – Parental qualification

The effects of the treatments (Table 4.9), shows that the different parental educational sub-groups were not significant in any case. So the null hypothesis is accepted, both in the case of changing attitudes and their retentivity.

5.4. CONCLUSIONS

The following conclusions are drawn from the study.

- Verbal-visual communication and dramatized-multimedia (film strips) communication and Integrated communication would all be quite effective -though with some variation in the effects -in producing attitude change, if the strategy, materials and programme of presentation are planned with purpose and care, and organized with adequate attention, exploiting their respective potential for cognitive and affective appeal.
- The forms or modes of communication and appeal by themselves would not perhaps be as important in producing attitude change, as the cognitive and affective contents that go into the presentation and the conviction they carry. The direct cognitive appeal and the instructional and persuasive effect of verbal-visual communication with purposefully selected content, good structure and forceful presentation could be as effective as dramatized-multimedia methods with their direct (affective) appeal and their entertainment effects which sometimes might override the instructional effects, unless handled with intelligent control.

- There seemed to be no difference between boys and girls in respect of the attitude as they existed.
- The middle SES group seemed to be middle in their positive attitude to manual work, casteism and family planning all the three attitudes. The middle group had highly significant difference from the low-group in respect of all the three attitudes. Thus no uniform trend or clear relationship was seen, except that the middle SES group was the most deviant and the poorest in respect of two attitudes while the low SES group was the poorest in respect of casteism.
- In the study of the effect of the treatment on the demographic sub groups (rural, urban), the attitude change induced in the urban groups towards casteism was retained significantly even after six months-where as none of the other sub groups vis a vis their attitudes, did not register any significant change. It is suggested that a separate study highlighting this particular aspect may be undertaken.
- In the study of the effects of the treatment on the religious sub-groups (Hindu, Muslim, Christian) has thrown up interesting criteria – that the Muslim group was perceptual to changes in attitude towards manual work and family planning and its retention. While Christian group persuasive enough to register higher gains (if not significant) in their attitude change towards 'casteism' and its retention, where as there is no such indication regarding Hindu groups. This interesting aspect could be probed further.
- In the study of the effects of the three treatments in producing and retention the attitude change, none of the parental qualification sub-groups differed – indicating that they are equally persuasive.
- On the whole as for the retentivity of attitude change is concerned, we can safely conclude that after a six months gap, the change in the attitudes was retained. Further longitudinal studies are suggested with varying intervals.

5.5. EDUCATIONAL IMPLICATIONS OF THE STUDY

- The experimental treatments in this project were conceived, planned and organized within a framework of strengths and weaknesses - with limitations inherent in the investigator any one person for that matter. The human and material resources he could master though he tried to do his best in this regard and the situation involvement of outside personnel, as communicators, student perception of the programme as extracurricular activities, time for the session and the spread of the programme, organizational facilities, made available to an outside agency, etc.

- There is scope simply scope for improvement in the planning, materials production, and organization phases of the programme.
- It would only be reasonable then, to expect that better programme would yield higher gains, and all the strategies and activities tried out are very suitable for normal school setting and programmes as curricular or co-curricular activities; they have also been found to be quite productive and promising.
- They have to be planned and organized on a wider scale in all schools.
- Teachers have to be prepared for this role of change agents in respect of healthy social attitudes through well-conceived and adequate components in the pre-service and in-service teacher training.
- It would also be advantage to us to produce materials of all kinds required for such programmes in a centralized way.

So if the school system accepts the development of healthy social attitudes and production of significant changes in them in desired direction, as an important part of its function, it could - and should - plan and organize such activities in a concerted way as an integral part of its total programme and that should make education more interesting and more socially relevant and useful.

5.6. SUGGESTIONS FOR FURTHER RESEARCH

- Schools could perform their function of healthy attitude development better, if they select more of socially relevant and important attitudes, and plan programme components with a combination strategy of direct visual-verbal communication, dramatized-multimedia and ICT communication, etc. As integral part of the curriculum and organize them with greater concentration, instead of touching upon them indirectly at several points, the latter approach could at best supplement and support the concentrated, purposeful effort.
- Teacher education programmes should emphasize the attitude development/change function of education and train teachers in organizing interesting and instructive programmes that bring substantial cognitive and affective change through direct and indirect appeal.

- Further research could be conducted, evolving more of clearly defined single-track strategies, multi-media, ICT and combination strategies, and substantive programmes adopting such strategies, and trying them out with adequate experimental control on secondary school and college students, with larger and more representative samples pooled from different geographical areas and socioeconomic strata, in respect of a wide range of social attitudes.

APPENDICES

APPENDIX A

A1 – THE VISAM SCALE

1. Name of the Student :
2. Name of the Father / Guardian :
3. Parental Occupation & Qualification:
4. Annual Income of the parent:
5. Name of the School:
6. Native Place :
7. Stay in the Village / Town more than one year :

S.No.	Direction	Statement	
1	-	All manual work must be eliminated through mechanization.	A B C D E
2	-	Cleaning vessels and plates and washing clothes are low jobs.	A B C D E
3	-	All kinds of kitchen work must be left to servants or to women who are not otherwise employed.	A B C D E
4	+	No one should consider it below his dignity to sweep, clean or tidy one's place.	A B C D E
5	-	Construction of roads, cleaning slums, sanitary maintenance, etc. are for paid labourers only.	A B C D E
6	+	It is natural for any one to carry his own shopping bags.	A B C D E
7	-	Manual work is to be done only by labourers or poor people	A B C D E
8	+	Every one must take part in social service camps including manual work.	A B C D E
9	+	One must learn to do all small repairs to cycle, scooters , etc., and to home appliances.	A B C D E
10	+	Working in one's garden is not below one's dignity whether it is flower garden or kitchen garden.	A B C D E
11	-	It is a shame if others see us cleaning or sweeping at home.	A B C D E
12	-	Peons or servants must be employed to shift chairs, benches, etc. in schools, colleges, whenever necessary.	A B C D E
13	+	Students of each class must be made responsible for cleaning their class rooms	A B C D E
14	-	Educated people should not be required to undertake manual work to earn living.	A B C D E
15	+	People should not lookdown upon any job as long as a it is socially useful and productive.	A B C D E

16	-	Persons who go on pionic should not be expected to clean plates or to carry the required things.	A B C D E
17	-	One should rather starve than to do jobs below one's dignity.	A B C D E
18	-	Labourers who do manual work look dirty and low.	A B C D E
19	+	Hobbies are respectable even when they involve manual work.	A B C D E
20	+	It gives us satisfaction if we can do most of our jobs involving manual work.	A B C D E
21	+	The educated unemployed should not hesitate to take up jobs like selling newspapers, shop-keeping, painting, household auto rickshaws, etc.,	A B C D E
22	-	Workers must be employed for jobs like whitewashing, painting, household repairs and improvements.	A B C D E
23	-	It is below the dignity of students to do manual work.	A B C D E
24	+	Every one should know how to stitch buttons, mend clothes and iron clothes.	A B C D E
25	+	Any job is respectable as long as it does not involve illegal and anti-social activities.	A B C D E
26	+	Blue color jobs (involving manual work) make as valuable contribution to the society and the nation, as white collar jobs.	A B C D E
27	+	Work experiences involving manual work should be a part of school curriculum.	A B C D E
28	-	Generally lablourers, rickshaw pullers, etc., who do manual work are not honest.	A B C D E
29	+	People who do manual work are healthy and strong.	A B C D E
30	-	We do not feel like doing any job when functions like marriages are celebrated in our house.	A B C D E

	A	B	C	D
+				
-				

Note :

Strongly Agree (A) Agree (B) - Neutral (C) - Disagree (D) - Strongly Disagree (E)

A2: The VISAC Scale

Sl.No	Direction	Statement	
1.	+	No person's worth depends upon his caste.	A B C D E
2.	+	Deciding the status of a person in society, by birth, is not correct.	A B C D E
3	-	The caste system in India has a sound and meaningful basis	A B C D E
4.	+	For long, the lower castes were not given reasonable social opportunities.	A B C D E
5.	+	For sometime to come persons belonging to 'lower castes' should be given special opportunities.	A B C D E
6.	-	Caste system not only shapes but strengthens our social structure.	A B C D E
7.	-	School and colleges run by different communities must give preference to the members of the respective communities.	A B C D E
8.	+	Caste should not be considered at all in giving seats in schools and colleges.	A B C D E
9.	+	Allotment of seats and jobs on the basis of caste goes against national interest.	A B C D E
10.	+	Merit should be the main consideration in deciding admissions, selection and promotions and not caste.	A B C D E
11.	+	Caste should not play any role in elections.	A B C D E
12.	-	Each caste has its due place and a special role to play in society.	A B C D E
13.	+	For centuries the 'lower' castes had been suppressed and exploited.	A B C D E
14.	-	It is natural for people to prefer persons of the same caste for company.	A B C D E
15.	-	Every caste should have representation on all important bodies of Government and in each office and factory.	A B C D E
16.	+	People of different castes must be encouraged to live in the same locality	A B C D E
17.	-	Friendship within the same caste would tend to be more intimate and durable.	A B C D E
18.	-	It is very comfortable to have many families of one's own caste in one's own neighbourhood.	A B C D E
19.	+	We must mix freely with others – irrespective of their caste	A B C D E
20.	-	We should invite people of own caste or certain selected castes only to any function in our house.	A B C D E
21.	+	Caste should not come in the way of selecting or choosing one's marriage partner.	A B C D E
22.	+	Children should be encouraged to mix freely with all without caste consideration.	A B C D E
23.	+	Social functions in which people participate without consideration of caste or creed must be encouraged.	A B C D E
24	-	It is but natural if people prefer to caste their votes in of candidates belongs to their caste.	A B C D E

25.	-	We should carefully teach our children all the habits and customs of our caste.	A B C D E
26.	+	Inter caste marriages should be promoted with incentives	A B C D E
27.	-	Each caste must try to preserve its identity and promote the special features of its culture.	A B C D E
28.	+	Education should help people to rise above petty caste considerations.	A B C D E
29.	-	If caste is given no prominence in every sphere, social integration is impossible	A B C D E
30.	-	There is nothing wrong in trying to bring a person of our caste into power by hook or crooks.	A B C D E

	A	B	C	D
+				
-				

A3: The VISAF Scale

S.No.	Direction	Statement	
1	-	More children in a family means more income for the family future.	A B C D E
2	+	Restricting the size of each family would serve national interest.	A B C D E
3	-	God gives us children and he would show the means to bring them up.	A B C D E
4	-	The larger the population the better will it be for defending the country.	A B C D E
5	+	If we do not interest our population ,we shall soon be with out food for many.	A B C D E
6	+	Religion should not come in the way of limiting the size of a family.	A B C D E
7	-	Family planning methods are artificial ,so they are injurious to health.	A B C D E
8	+	Parents with many children cannot afford to give them all good higher education.	A B C D E
9	-	Family planning is against the laws of nature and god ,so it should not be followed.	A B C D E
10	-	Each family should have more sons than daughters whatever may be the total number.	A B C D E

11	-	More children would mean more security for parents in old age.	A B C D E
12	+	A small family helps to maintain good standard of living.	A B C D E
13	+	Parents may not consider their children as a burden but they add to the burden of the society.	A B C D E
14	+	The more the increase in population the more difficult it will be to get jobs.	A B C D E
15	-	Knowledge of birth control methods would tend to lower the moral standards of people.	A B C D E
16	-	More people in country would mean more capacity to produce goods or wealth	A B C D E
17	+	Increase in population causes scarcity in essential commodities.	A B C D E
18	+	Increased production will result in better standard of living if only we control population growth.	A B C D E
19	-	The bigger the family the merrier the company.	A B C D E
20	+	The more the number of children in a family the smaller would be the savings.	A B C D E
21	+	More children in a family would mean smaller of the family property, so we should restrict our family.	A B C D E
22	+	The longer the population ,the more difficult will be the housing problem.	A B C D E
23	+	The more the mouths to be fed in a family the more severe is the problem of meeting the essential needs.	A B C D E
24	-	Family planning methods are not consistent with Indian culture ,so they should not be followed.	A B C D E
25	+	If necessary ,a law should be passed in order restrict the size of each family.	A B C D E
26	-	Our ansisters belived that 'if there is no son,there is no heaven'- this is true.	A B C D E
27	-	More male children would mean more earnings through dowry – so we should have as many as possible.	A B C D E
28	-	Family planning methods are injurious to health –so they should not be practiced.	A B C D E

	A	B	C	D
+				
-				

A4–SOCIO-ECONOMIC STATUS SCALE

Research Director
Dr. Nimma Venkata Rao
Professor & Head
Andhra University
Department of Education
VISAKHAPATNAM
Andhra University, VISAKHAPATNAM

Research Scholar
R S S Nehru
Department of Education
M.A. (Phil.), M.A. (Edn.) Ph.D.

Name of the Student______________________________

Class ______________________ **Section**____________________

Date of Birth_______________

House Address

____

____

Instructions

Your family's socio-economic status with be studied by the use of this scale. You are requested to read carefully and put a (√) mark in the brackets opposite to each statement. All the particulars are kept secret, so you can fill in with out any doubt.

Authorized Version of

Prof. R. A. Singh
Psychology Department
Jagadamba College, Chapra (Bihar)
and
Prof. S.K. Saxena
Education Department
D.B.S. College, Kanpur
Agra Psychology Research Cell (APRC)
Tiwari Kothi, Belananj – 282004 (India)

1	The educational qualifications of the members of your family are	Father guardian	Mother	Education brother	Education sister
A.	Highest (Ph.D, MS, MD etc)	( )	( )	( )	( )
B.	P.G. (MA, M.Sc etc)	( )	( )	( )	( )
C.	Degree (BA., B.Com, B.Sc.)	( )	( )	( )	( )
D.	Higher Secondary (inter, PDc)	( )	( )	( )	( )
E.	Middle School (pass in viii)	( )	( )	( )	( )
F.	Primary level (pass in v)	( )	(.)	( )	( )
G.	Literates (can read and write)	( )	( )	( )	( )
H.	Illiterates	( )	( )	( )	( )

2	Occupations of your family members officer highest level officer	Father guardian	Mother	Education brother	Education sister
A.	Manager, principle etc	( )	( )	(·)	( )
B.	Middle level officer	( )	( )	( )	( )
C.	Ordinary/ job /clerk teacher	( )	( )	( )	( )
D.	Skilled job carpenter etc	( )	( )	( )	( )
E.	Middle level person (typist PA,PS) skilled person /peon watchman /worker)	( )	( )	( )	( )
F.	Middle level skilled person peon watchman worker	( )	( )	( )	( )
G.	Ordinary servant (coolie/ watchman /rickshaw-puller)s	( )	( )	( )	( )

3. The Income of your family per month in Rupees is_______

A) >1501 ( )
B) Between 1001 & 1500 ( )
C) Between 501 & 1000 ( )
D) Between 201 & 500 ( )
E) Between 101 & 200 ( )
F) Less than or Equal to 100 ( )

4. Credits and Debts of your family in Rupees _______

A) >1500 ( )
B) Between 1001 & 1500 ( )
C) Between 501 & 1000 ( )
D) Between 201 & 500 ( )
E) Between 101 & 200 ( )
F) Less than or Equal to 100 ( )

5. In emergency, how much money can your family could collect (in Rupees)

A) >1501 ( )
B) Between 1001 & 1500 ( )
C) Between 501 & 1000 ( )
D) Between 201 & 500 ( )
E) Between 101 & 200 ( )
F) Less than or Equal to 100 ( )

6. The house you live in is ________
A) Own ( )
B) Own but half of if rented ( )
C) Rented ( )
D) Left own house living rented ( )

7. Type of the house living in _____
A) Big bungalow with garden current & Phone ( )
B) Small Bunglow, with garden & current ( )
C) Phase Permanent Structure with current ( )
D) Small Permanent Structure with current ( )
E) Tin Shed, earthen / floor / cement ( )
F) Hut with earthen floor ( )

8. Put a ✓ mark in brackets provided after each item ________
A) Car ( ), Auto ( ), Motor Bike ( ), Cycle ( )
B) Stereo ( ), TV ( ), CD Player ( ), Radio ( )
C) Fridge ( ), Colour ( ), Steel Almirah ( ), Iron Almirah ( ), Dining Table ( ), Steel Plates & Glasses ( )
D) Sofa set ( ), Good Table / Chair ( ), Modern Chairs ( )
E) Ordinary Table / Chair ( ), Wall Clock ( ), Whist Watch ( )
F) Gas Stove ( ), Current Stove ( ), Pressure Cooker ( ), Water Boiler ( ), Kesotine Stove ( )
G) Mixie ( ), Electric Automatic iron ( ),Grinder ( ),Sewing machine ( )
H) Camera ( ), Tea-Set ( ), Glass Set ( ), Picnic Set ( )

9. What type of magazines your family read
A) Daily ( )
B) Weekly ( )
C) Monthly ( )
D) Quarterly ( )
E) Occasional Purchase ( )
F) Never Read ( )

10. Your family spends how much on news papers per month in rupees____
A) 10 ( )
B) 20 ( )
C) 30 ( )
D) 50 ( )

11. In the opinion of your family members who think that casteism should be there
A) Father ( )
B) Mother ( )
C) Guardian ( )
D) Elder Brother ( )
E) Elder Sister ( )

12. Maximum stay of my family was in _____

A)	Posh are with cars / phone	( )
B)	Middle class locality	( )
C)	Ordinary class locality `	( )
D)	Locality Daily wage earners who doubt earn when there is no job	( )

13. Do your family members think that religion and caste are the essential factors to do social service ?

A)	Yes	( )
B)	NO	( )
C)	Some Time	( )

14. Do your family members are members of any religion social / caste group

A)	Yes	( )
B)	NO	( )

15. Do your family members take part in the functions of the society / locality

A)	Always	( )
B)	Some Times	( )
C)	Never	( )

16. The elders of your family keep relationships with the following

A)	Religion / Caste groups	( )
B)	Equal Status	( )
C)	Politicians	( )
D)	Neigbourers	( )

17. The people living in your locality have the following impression on your / your family

A)	Very rich following	( )
B)	Rich	( )
C)	Middle Class	( )
D)	Ordinary Class	( )
E)	Lower Class	( )

18. For the Social status enjoyed by your family the reason is _____

A)	Your Profession / Work	( )
B)	Your Property / Economic Status	( )
C)	Your religion	( )

APPENDIX B

TREATMENT MATERIAL

MANUAL WORK

B-1.1.	**Reading and comprehension Exercise (T_1 and T_3)**	
	Focus on	Time in Mts.
(a)	A Passage highlighting i. Meaning of manual work ii. Views of great thinkers iii. Advantages of cultivating hobbies involving manual work. iv. Conclusion -- stressing that one should not hesitate to indulge in activities involving manual work.	30
(b)	Exercise: 5 True -- False items	5
(c)	Interaction and summing up	10
	Total	45 Mts.

B-1.2	**Self –instructional material (T_1 and T_3)**	Time in Mts.
	Focus on	
(a)	Preview	
(b)	Dignity of labour – highlighting the point that any work involving Labour is dignified as long as it is not against social interest.	
(c)	Advantages of manual work	30
	At the end of every frame and at the end of the material response self -- check items (true -- false type, completion type) were given	5
(d)	Interaction and conclusion	10
	Total	45 Mts.

B-1.3. Talk on manual work (T_1)

The talk on manual work was delivered highlighting the following.

	Focus on	Aids	Time in Mts.
(a)	Concept of manual work	-	5
(b)	Dignity of labour Views of great thinkers i. Gandhiji ii. Iswarachandra Vidyasagar	Chart showing Raja Ranajit Singh helping an old woman by carrying her basket.	15
(c)	Value of social service campus and activates	Chart showing a road – construction activity of students.	5
(d)	Importance of cultivating	Chart (1): Showing a man repairing his own cycle. Chart (2): Showing a fresh unemployed graduate – and a lot of job opportunities for him, if he does not mind accepting jobs that involve manual work	10
(e)	Interaction and summing up		10
		Total	45 Mts.

B-1.4: Panel discussion (T_1)

A panel discussion was presented involving two persons role – playing as director employment services and director of social services and welfare of the government of Andhra Pradesh. It covered the following points.

	focus on	Time in Mts.
(a)	Problem of un-employment - causes – like disinclination on the part of some young men to take up jobs involving manual work.	10
(b)	Ours is called 'Computers Age' – in spite of heavy mechanization man should remain the master and also do many things himself.	10
(c)	Importance of the programme – "Earn-While – you – Learn" as adopted by some advanced countries and there is need in our society also for programmes like that.	5
(d)	Concept of dignity of labour and its importance.	10
(e)	Interaction and conclusion.	10
	Total	45 Mts.

B-1.6 Mono-acting (T_2 and T_3)

The roles played were those of (1) a highly placed corrupt official and (2) a rich lady erroneously abusing her maid – servant for lost ornaments.

	Focus on	Aids	Time in Mts
(a)	Rama Rao and rickshaw puller.	Tape – recorded conversation between the officers and the rickshaw – puller after reaching his house – bound brief case missing – after the rickshaw went away – abused the puller (who was not there – expressed his dislike for such) rickshaw – puller came back – handed over brief case – refused reward – claims that he did his duty only – went away.	10
	ii. Rama Rao got that money, as a bribe shocked at the honesty of the rickshaw – puller – forced to compare himself with the rickshaw puller – felt ashamed – declares his impression about manual workers as erroneous – decided to live honestly.		10
(b)	Lakshmi Devi and Sita Lakshmi Devi Rick house – used to harass her servant, Sita – sita was dismissed – threatened lakshmi devi discovered the chain later – regrets – called sita back – sita refused – a lady of self – respect.	Tape recorded background depicting the harsh nature of lakshmi Devi – excessive work entrusted.	20
		Total	45 Mts.

	Focus on	Aids	Time in Mts.
(a)	The situation played was the interaction between the Managing director of a factory and labour – leader in a factory – strike situation. The workers went on rampage – a section of them resorted to sabotage – fie – striking workers them selves – fought with fire – put it out – suffering and sacrifices – on their part – valuable property saved - compromise mooted – management conceded to their demands – labourers offered to surrender some of the benefits (for six months) in view of the damage caused by the fire.	Tape recorded sound effects of a strike scene – fire putting it out.	40
(b)	Interaction and conclusion		5
		Total	45 Mts.

	Focus on	Aids	Time in Mts
(a)	The plot dealt with a rich brother and his sister. He came home frustrated – cause was breakdown of his motor-bike near his village farm where he went – described to his sister the stupid mean – looking rogue of a lorry driver who refused to help him (of course due to his own arrogance only) – sister pointed out the truth – advised him to learn the basics of repair – told him of the advantages of manual work – brother relaised its importance – promised her.	Tape recorded break – down scene sounds – dialogue between brother and lorry – driver.	40
(b)	Interaction and conclusion		5
		Total	45 Mts.

Dramatized –multimedia strategy

B- 3.8: Film strips on manual work (T_2 and T_3)

Film strips on manual work was shown which highlights:

Sl.No.	Focus On	Time in Mts
1	**Interdiction about manual work and importance**	5
2	**Video and cinema clip on** Conversation between two friends- Sailash and Sarath that - cleaning vessels and plates and washing clothes are low jobs - show live video.	3
3	**Video and cinema clip on** Conversation between two boys Ram and Lakshman- All kinds of kitchen work must be left to servants or to women who are not otherwise employed- show live video.	3
4	**Video and cinema clip on** Conversation between group of friends- That no one should consider it below his dignity to sweep, clean or tidy one's place- and construction of roads, cleaning slums, sanitary maintenance, etc. are for paid laborers only- show live video.	3
5	**Video and cinema clip on** -It is natural for any one to carry his own shopping bags - Persons who go on picnic should not be expected to clean plates or to carry the required things.	3
6	**Video and cinema clip on** Every one must take part in social service camps including manual work.	3
7	**Video and cinema clip on** One must learn to do all small repairs to cycle, scooters, etc., and to home appliances-working in one's garden is not below one's dignity whether it is flower garden or kitchen garden.	3
8	**Show the live video tape on** -it is a shame if others see us cleaning or sweeping at home.	3
9	**Show the live video tape from Prof. Viswam** Peons or servants must be employed to shift chairs, benches, etc. in schools, colleges, whenever necessary-Students of each class must be made responsible for cleaning their class rooms.	3
10	**Video /cinema clip on from** Educated people should not be required to undertake manual work to earn living. People should not lookdown upon any job as long as a it is socially useful and productive.	3
11	**Video /cinema clip from Jeans** We never felt that "one should rather starve than to do jobs below one's dignity"- so The educated unemployed should not hesitate to take up jobs like selling newspapers, shop-keeping, painting, household auto rickshaws, etc.,	3
12	**Video /cinema clip on** Hobbies are respectable even when they involve manual work.	3
13	**Video /cinema clip on** It gives us satisfaction if we can do most of our jobs involving manual work.	3

14	**Video /cinema clip on** It is below the dignity of students to do manual work-Workers must be employed for jobs like whitewashing, painting, household repairs and improvements-Every one should know how to stitch buttons, mend clothes and iron clothes.	3
15	**Video /cinema clip on** Any job is respectable as long as it does not involve illegal and anti-social activities.	3
16	**Video /cinema clip on** Generally lablourers, rickshaw pullers, etc., who do manual work are not honest. Blue color jobs (involving manual work) make as valuable contribution to the society and the nation, as white collar jobs.	3
17	**Video /cinema clip on** People who do manual work are healthy and strong.	3
18	**Video /cinema clip on** We do not feel like doing any job when functions like marriages are celebrated in our house.	3
19	**Video /cinema clip on** Work experiences involving manual work should be a part of school curriculum.	7
Total		**60 Mts**

B-2 Casteism

B-2.1: Reading and comprehension exercise (T_1 and T_3)

	Focus on	Aids	Time Mts
(a)	A passage highlighting: i. Origin of castes – manmade – based on profession. ii. Change in social structure but caste system remained. iii. Exploitation of lower castes. iv. Remedial measures		30
(b)	Exercise: Seven completion type question.		5
(c)	Interaction and summing up		10
		Total	45 Mts.

B-2.2. Self -instructional material (T_1 and T_3)

	Focus on	Time Mts.
(a)	i. Preview ii. Casteism is not good for our society. iii. Suggestions to get rid of it. At the end of every frame and at the end of the material response self – check items (true – false type and completion type) were given.	30 5
(b)	Interaction and summing up.	10
	Total	45 Mts.

B-1.3. Talk on casteism (T_1)

The talk highlighted

	Focus on	Aids	Time in Mts.
(a)	Concept of the caste system – social evil.	Chart showing four persons belonging to Brahmin, Kshatriya, Vysya and Shudra in their typical dresses.	10
(b)	Changing society.		10
(c)	Exploitation by some selfish people.		5
(d)	How it could be put an end to.		10
(e)	Interaction and summing up.		10
		Total	45 Mts.

B-2.4: Panel discussion on casteism (T_1)

Two persons, playing the roles of Dr. P. Rama Rao, Head of the Department of Sociology of Andhra University and Shri V.D. Murthy, famous social worker, discus sex the following points.

	Focus on	Aids	Time in Mts.
(a)	Irrelevance of caste concept in the present day society.	Chart showing bramins prohibiting harijans using the same well to get water.	5
(b)	Un-touchability and its social implications.		10
(c)	Part played by casteism in our election system.		5
(d)	Steps for the eradication of the evil of casteism.	Chart highlighting the salient points.	10
(e)	Problems of inter – caste marriages.	Chart showing an intercaste marriage.	10
(f)	Interaction and summing up.		10
		Total	45 Mts.

B-2.6: Mono-acting on casteism (T_2 and T_3)

	Focus on	Aids	Time in Mts.
(a)	Introduction	Tape recorded poll campaign scene vote for – vote for – the symbol being 'fox' the shouts were for the victory for fox, etc., gradually they approached a house. Knocking sound – requested for soliciting his vote went away.	5
(b)	Reflections of the gentleman, Rama Sastri – last same – he felt cheated – the same Brahmin candidate stood for election in their municipal ward – appealed to Ramasastry's caste feelings – got elected – did nothing for the ward – made money – showing his face only at the next elections – Rama Sastry – this time decided to shed the caste considerations – realized mistake – wanted to vote to Chinnaswamy – though he did not belong to his caste – Thus to uphold the value of vote – beyond the petty caste – level.		30
(c)	Interaction and conclusion		10
		Total	45 Mts.

B-2.7: Play -- let on casteism (T_2)

Focus on	Aids	Time in Mts.
A busy road junction scene – a well – known one in Visakhapatnam – Lorry accident – Brahmin got knocked – public sympathy – cobbler with his shop just opposite – helped the old man – took to hospital – donated blood – saved him (this was presented as flash – back as retold by the old – man).	Audio --effects of an accident.	5
Cobbler went to the old Brahmin's house – oldman treated him as an equal – cobbler felt un-easy – old man spelt out his new - found realism – all castes are man – made – but all are same in the eyes of god – blood same – his own living example – cursed himself for his ignorance throughout the past - lived as a good friend f the cobbler.		30
Interaction and summing up.		10
	Total	45 Mts.

B-2.8: Skit on casteism (T_2 and T_3)

	Focus on	Time in Mts.
(a)	Heated discussion between Radha, orthodox – rich – elder sister – and – Hari young brother of modern views – regarding his marrying the girl of his choice – a girl from low caste – Hari put across his views – meaningless clinging to caste asked her reasons – countered them with his reasonable arguments – convinced her – won here approval.	35
(b)	Interaction and summing up.	10
	Total	45 Mts.

Dramatized – multimedia strategy

B- 3.8: Film strips on casteism (T_2 and T_3)

Film strips on casteism was shown which highlights:

S.No.	Focus on	Time in Mts
1	**Shows the song from Osai ramulamma** Interdiction to caste system in India - how it was prevalent .	6
2	**Video /cinema clip on : Subha sankalpam** Foreign delegates-with yerrodu (an uneducated –country fisher man)-talk about acconts- Yerrodu without computer –give correct date to the delegates.	4
3	**Video /cinema clip on** For centuries the 'lower' castes had been suppressed and exploited -for sometime to come persons belonging to 'lower castes' should be given special opportunities- School and colleges run by different communities must give preference to the members of the respective communities-Caste should not be considered at all in giving seats in schools and colleges-allotment of seats and jobs on the basis of caste goes against national interest.	5
4	**Video /cinema clip on :Okav okkadu** It is natural for people to prefer persons of the same caste for company-each caste has its due place and a special role to play in society-there is nothing wrong in trying to bring a person of our caste into power by hook or crooks- it is but natural if people prefer to caste their votes in of candidates belongs to their caste-caste should not play any role in elections.	15
5	**Video /cinema clip on** Every caste should have representation on all important bodies of Government and in each office and factory-People of different castes must be encouraged to live in the same locality -Friendship within the same caste would tend to be more intimate and durable-It is very comfortable to have many families of one's own caste in one's own neighborhood-We must mix freely with others – irrespective of their caste.	3
6	**Video /cinema clip on** Caste should not come in the way of selecting or choosing one's marriage partner.	3
7	**Video /cinema clip on** Social functions in which people participate without consideration of caste or creed must be encouraged.	3
8	**Video /cinema clip on** Children should be encouraged to mix freely with all without caste consideration-We should carefully teach our children all the habits and customs of our caste-Inter caste marriages should be promoted with incentives-Each caste must try to preserve its identity and promote the special features of its culture-Education should help people to raise above petty caste considerations.	6
9	**Video /cinema clip on** If caste is given no prominence in every sphere, social integration is impossible.	3
	Interaction and summing up.	10
	Total	60

B-3. Family planning

B-3.1. Reading and comprehension Exercise (T_1 and T_3)

	Focus on	**Time in Mts.**
(a)	A passage highlighting i. Family planning – one of the most difficult problems faced by India. ii. Our economic growth is off – set by the population growth. iii. Population explosion – concept.	30
(b)	Five simple questions that require the answer to be written in one or two sentences in the space provided were given.	5
(c)	Interaction and summing up.	10
	Total	45 Mts.

B-3.2. Self – Instructional Material (T_1 and T_3)

	Focus on	**Time in Mts.**
(a)	i. Preview ii. Advantage of 'small family' iii. Disadvantage of 'Large family' iv. Meaning of 'Population Explosion'. v. Role of family planning in developing our nation. At the end of every frame and at the end of the material response self – check items (true – false and completion type) were given.	30 5
(b)	Interaction and Conclusions.	10
	Total	45 Mts.

B-3.3: Talk on family planning (T_1)

The talk high lighted.

	Focus on	Aids	Time in Mts.
(a)	i. Tremendous population growth and its impact on social and economic areas. ii. The concept of family planning. iii. Advantage of family planning. iv. Advantages of a small family and disadvantages of a large family. v. Population explosion. vi. How to check the growth of population.	Chart depicting the growth rate of population. Chart listing out advantages. Chart pasteurizing population explosion. Chart giving the salient points.	5 5 5 5 10
(b)	Interaction and summing up.		10
		Total	45 Mts.

B-3.4: Panel discussion on family planning (T_1)

Two people, playing the roles of director of family planning, Government of Andhra Pradesh and superintendent, K.G. Hospital discussed the following points.

	Focus on	Aids	Time in Mts.
(a)	i. What is family planning programme? ii. Factors that come in the way of the family planning programme. 1. Religious beliefs. 2. Other superstitions 3. Social evils (dowry system, child marriages) iii. How to overcome them? iv. If successful in implementing the family planning programme what are the benefits? v. If not checked, what will be the disastrous consequences?	Chart listing the factors. Chart listing the disastrous effects.	5 10 5 5 10
(b)	Interaction and summing up		10
		Total	45 Mts.

B- 3.5. : Play – let on family planning (T_3)

	Focus on	Aids	Time in Mts.
(a)	Introduction	i. 10 charts ii. Family planning 2 models. iii. Tape recorded audio-effects of a family – planning exhibition in K.G. medical college.	5
(b)	Ravi and Gopi, Two IX std. students of AVN College high school planning exhibition organized in K.G. Medical College. Ravi is from a small family while Gopi is one of the seven children of his family. Ravi wants to play a game in the exhibition but Gopi did not have any money. He was in a sulky mood. Ravi asked for the reason – they exchanged confidences and advantages of a small family and disadvantages of a large family – both agreed that having a small family is advantageous.		30
(c)	Interaction and summing up.		10
		Total	45 Mts.

B- 3.6. Mono action on family planning (T_2 and T_3)

	Focus on	Aids	Time in Mts.
(a)	Introduction Flash back of a situation 10 years back in Sekhar's life.	i. Marriage atmosphere – tape recorded – doctor friend of groom advised the couple to have a small family – ignored. ii. Another taped situation of the present day situation in Sekhar 's house – sick wife, fighting children, cries, demands for fees, etc.,	10
(b)	Sekhar enters – cries over split milk – broods over his present problems traces them back to his stupid ness in not observing the 'small family' norm – never too late – determines to go back to his doctor friend.		25
(c)	Interaction and summing up.		10
		Total	45 Mts.

Dramatized--multimedia strategy

B- 3.8: Film strips on family planning (T_2 and T_3)

Film strips on family planning was shown which highlights:

B- 3.8: Film on family planning (T_2 and T_3)

S.No	Focus on	Time in Mts
1	Movie song from -**Tata manvadu** On family planning and population growth- and problems.	6
2	**Video /cinema clip on** More children in a family mean more income for the family future-Restricting the size of each family would serve national interest-A small family helps to maintain good standard of living-Parents with many children cannot afford to give them all good higher education.	5
3	**Video /cinema clip on** God gives us children and he would show the means to bring them up-Religion should not come in the way of limiting the size of a family-More children would mean more security for parents in old age.	4
4	**Video /cinema clip on** The larger the population the better will if be for defending the country.	3
5	**Video /cinema clip from Akali rajayam** If we do not interest our population, we shall soon be without food for many.	2
6	**Video /cinema clip on** Family planning methods are artificial, so they are injurious to health -Family planning is against the laws of nature and god, so it should not be followed. Knowledge of birth control methods would tend to lower the moral standards of people-Family planning methods are not consistent with Indian culture, so they should not be followed- Family planning methods are injurious to health -so they should not be practiced.	7
7	**Video /cinema clip from Kalikalam** Our ansisters belived that 'if there is no son, there is no heaven'- this is true-Each family should have more sons than daughters whatever may be the total number.	9
8	**Video /cinema clip from Akali rajayam** The more the increase in population the more difficult it will be to get jobs-Increase in population causes scarcity in essential commodities-Increased production will result in better standard of living if only we control population growth-More people in country would mean more capacity to produce goods or wealth-The longer the population, the more difficult will be the housing problem.	15
9	**Video /cinema clip on** The more the number of children in a family the smaller would be the savings-More children in a family would mean smaller of the family property, so we should restrict our family-More male children would mean more earnings through dowry – so we should have as many as possible.	4
	Video /cinema clip on The more the mouths to be fed in a family the more severe is the problem of meeting the essential needs-If necessary, a law should be passed in order restrict the size of each family.	5
Total		60

BIBLIOGRAPHY

Ableson. K.P. and G-.S, Lesser (1959). A development theory of persuasibility. In I.L. Jomis and C.I. Hovland (Eds.), *Personality and. Persuasibility.* New Haven: Yale Univ. Press.

Ableson. R.P. and M.J. Rosenberg (1958). Symbolic Psychologic: a model of attitudinal cognition. Behav Sc., 3.

Ableson. R.P., E. Aronson. W.J. Me Guire. T.M. Newcomb, M.J. Rosenberg, and P.H. Tannenbaum (Eds.) (1968). Theories of cognitive consistency. A Source Book. Chicago: Rand Mc Nally.

Aderman, D. and S.S. Brehm (1976). on the recall of initial attitudes following counter – attitudinal advocacy: An experimental re-examination. *Pers. Soc. Psychol.*, 2.

Ahluwalia, S.P. (1978). A study of change in professional attitudes of student teachers. *J. Inst. Educ. Res.*, 2.

Alberta, S.E. and S. Siegel (1951). Reference groups, Membership groups, and attitude change. *J. Abnorm. Soc. Psychol.*, 55.

Alison Kelly (1986). The development of girls' and boys' attitudes to science: A longitudinal study, *International Journal of Science Education*, Volume 8, Issue 4 October 1986.

Allen V.L. and J.M. Levin (1971). Social support and conformity. The role of independent assessment of reality. *J. Exp. Soc. Psychol.*, 7.

Allport. G.W. (1935). Attitudes. In C. Murichson (Ed.), *Hand Book of Social Psychology*, Worcester, Mass: Clark Univ. Press.

Anant (1968). Attitude towards caste system in North India, III International Congress of Psychiatry, Yugoslavia, 1970. *The Hanging Concept of Caste in India.* Vikas Publishing House Pvt. Ltd., Delhi, 1972.

Anders, C Berg. R. (2005). Factors related to observed attitude change toward learning chemistry among university students, *Chem. Educ. Res. Pract.*, 2005, 6 (1).

Anderson, N.H. (1959). Test of a model of opinion change. *J. Abnorm. Soc. Psychol.*, 59.

Anderson, N.H. (1965). Primacy effects in personality impression formation using a generalized order effect paradigm. *J. Abnorm. Soc. Psychol.*, 2.

Anderson, N.H. (1976). Integration theory applied to cognitive responses and attitudes. In R.E. Petty, T.M Ostrom, T.C. Brock (Eds.) N.Y.: Mc Graw-hill.

Anderson, N.H. and A.A. Barrios (1961). Primacy effects in personality impression formation. JASP., 63.

Annis A.D. and N.C. Meier (1934). The induction of opinion through suggestions by means of 'planted content'. *J. Soc. Psychol.,* 5.

Aronson, E. (1966). Threat and Obedience. Transaction.

Aronson, E. and B.W. Golden (1962). Effect of relevant and irrelevant aspects of communicator credibility on attitude change. *J. Pers.*, 30.

Aronson, E. and J.M. Carlsmith (1963). Effect of the serverity of threat on the devaluation of forbidden behaviour *J. Abnorm. Soc. Psychol.,* 66.

Asch, S.E. (1952). Social Psychology. Englewood Cliffs. New Jersey: Prentice-Hall.

Asch. S.E. (1948). The doctrine of suggestion, prestige and imitation in Social Psychology. *Psychol. Rev.*, 55.

Asch. S.E. (1956). Studies of independence and conformity; a minority of one against a unanimous majority. *Psychol. Monogr.*, 70, No. 9 (whole No. 416).

Ball-Rokeach, S.J., Rokeach, M., & Grube, J.W. (1984). The great American values test. New York: Free Press.

Barber, T.X. and D.S. Calverley (1964). Hypnotizability, Suggestibility and personality; IV. A study with the Learly Interpersonal checklist. *Brit. J. Soc. Clin. Psychol.*, 3.

Bauer. R.A. (1965). A revised mode of source effect. Presidential address of consumer psychology. American psychological Association Annual Meeting, Chicago.

Beach, Rath. I. (1966). The effects of a 'fear – arousing' safety film on physiological attitudinal and behavioured measures; a pilot study 'Traffic Safety', *Res. Rev.*, 10.

Bednar, A. & Levie, W.H. (1993). Attitude-change principles. In M. Fleming & W.H. Levie (Eds.), Instructional message design: Principles from the behavioral and cognitive sciences (pp. 283-304). Englewood Cliffs, NJ: Educational Technology Publications.

Beighley, K.C. (1952). An experimental study of the effect of four speck variable of listener comprehension. *Speech Monogr.*, 19.

Beloff, H. (1958). Two forms of social conformity: acquiescence and conventionality, *J. Abnorm. Soc. Psychol.*, 56.

Beloson, W.A. (1956). Learning attitude change resulting from viewing a television series. 'Bon Voyage'. *Brit. J. Educ. Psychol.*, 26.

Belson, W.A. (1961). Communication and persuasion through broadcasting. Business Rev.

Bem, D.J. (1972). Self – Perception theory. In Advances in Experimental Social Psychology, New York: Academic Press, 6.

Bem, D.J., H.K. Mc Connel (1970). Testing the Self-perception of Dissonance phenomena on compliance of premanipulation attitudes. *J. Pers. Soc. Psychol.*, 14.

Bennett, E.B. (1955). Discussion, decision, commitment and consensus in "group decision". Hum. Relat., 8.

Berkowitz, L and D.R. Cottingham (1960). The interest value and relevance of fear arousing communication. *J. Abnorm. Soc. Psychol.*, 60.

Berkowitz, L.Y. and R.M. Lundy (1957). Personality characteristics related to susceptibility to influence by peers or authority figures. *J. Pers.*, 25.

Berlson, B., P.L. Lazarfeld, and W.N. Mc phee (1954). Voting, Chicago: Univ. of Chicago Press.

Bettinghaus, E.P. (1961). Operation of Congruity in an oral communication setting. *Speech Monogr.*, 28.

Bierbraher. G., Poss, L. and J. Hoffman (1973). The role of attribution processes in conformity and dissent. *Am. Psychol.*, 31.

Biggers, T., and P. Bert (1982). Attitude change: A function of emotion-eliciting qualities of environment. *Pers. Soc. Psychol.*,. Bull. 8 (1).

Bloom. B. S. (1964). Stability and Change in Human Characteristics. New York: Wiley.

Bogardus, E.S. (1928). Immigration and Race Attitudes. Boston: Health.

Bowers J.W. (1965). The influence of delivery on attitudes towards concepts and speakers. *Speech Monogr.* 32.

Bowers, J.W. (1964). Some correlates of language intensity. *Quart. J. Speech.* 50.

Bradac, J.J., C.W. Konsky and R.A. Davies (1976). Two studies of effects of linguistic diversity upon judgments of communicator attitudes and message effectiveness. *Commun. Monogr.* . 43.

Bradac, J.W. and M.M. Osborn (1966). Attitudinal effects of selected types of concluding metaphors in persuasive speech. *Speech Monogr.*, 33.

Breham, J. and A.R. Cohen (1962). Explorations in Cognitive Dissonance. New York: Wiley.

Brehm. J. and D. Lispher (1959). Communicator – communicates discrepancy and perceived communicator trustworthiness. *J. Pers.* 27.

Burdick, H. (1955). The Compliant behavior of deviates under conditions of threat. Doctoral dissertation, university of Minnesota.

Byrne. D. (1961). International attraction and attitude similarly. *J. Abnorm. Soc. Psychol.*, 62.

Byrne. D. and W. Griffitt (1966). A developmental investigation. *J. Pers. Soc. Psychol.*, 4.

Byrne. D., and D. Nelson (1964). Attraction as a function of attitude similarity – dissimilarity of attitudes.*J. Abnorm. Soc. Psychol.*, 65.

Caidar. B.J. (1974). Informational cues and attributions of attitudes *J. Exp. Soc. Psychol.*, 12.

Calder. B.J. H. Ross, and C.A, Insko (1973). Attitude change and attitude attribution: Effects of incentive, choice and consequences. *J. Pers. Soc. Psychol.*, 25.

Campbell D.T. (1950). The indirect assessment of social attitudes. *Psygeol. Bull*, 47.

Campbell. D.T. and R,A. Lavine (1965). ProposmiomsAbbots Ethnocentrism from Social Science Theories. Evanston, III. Department of Psychology, N.W. Univ.

Cantril. H. and G.W. All port (1935). The Psychology of Radio. New York. Harper.

Carmiohael. C.W., G.L. Crobkhite (1965). Frustration and language intensity. *Speech. Monogr.*, 32.

Carthy. J.D. and F.J. Ebling. (Eds.) (1964). The History of Aggression. New York: Academic Press.

Cartwright. D. (1949). Some principles of mass persuasion. *Hum. Relat.*, 2.

Chamberlin, T.C. (1965). The method of multiple working hypotheses. *Silence*, 148.

Chen W.K.C. (1936). Retention effects of oral propaganda. *J.Soc. Psychol.*, 7.

Chen, W.K.C. (1935). The influence of oral propaganda upon student attitudes. *Arch. Psychol.* (N.Y.) No. 150.

Cherrington, B.M. and L.W. Miller (1933). Change in attitude as a result of lecture and of reading similar material. *J. Soc. Psychol.*,7.

Cialdini, R.B., S.L., Braver, and S.K. Lewis (1976). Attribution bias and the easily persuaded others. *J. Abnorm. Soc. Psychol,* 30.

Cohen, A.R. (1959). Need for cognition and order of communication as a determinant of opinion change. In C.I. Hovland (Ed.,) Order of Presentation in Persuasion. New Haven: Yale Univ. Press.

Cook, S.W. and Claire Sellitz (1964). A multiple indicator approach to attitude measurement. *Psychol. Bull.*, 62.

Cooper E. and H. Dinerman (1951). Analysis of the film "Don't Be a Sucker": a study of communication. *Publ. Opin. Quart.* 15.

Cooper J., and S. Worchel (1970). Role of undesired consequences in arousing cognitive dissonance. *J. Pers. Soc. Psychol.,* 16.

Cooper J., M.P. Zenna and G.R. Goethals (1974). Mistreatment of an esteemed other as a consequence of affecting dissonance reduction. *J.Exp. Soc. Psychol.*, 10.

Cox, D.F. and R.A. Bower (1964). Self – confidence and persuasibility in women. *Publ. Opin. Quart.*, 28.

Cromwell., H. and R Kuchel (1952). An experimental study of the effect on attitude of listeners of repeating the same oral propaganda. *J. Soc. Psychol.*, 35.

Croucher, A. (1982). Age and sex differences, change in attitude toward junior school subjects during school year (9-11) year old students). *Psychological Abstractor,* Vol. 68, No. 6.

Crouter, Ann C et all., (2007). Development of Gender Attitude Traditionality Across Middle Childhood and Adolescence, *Child Development,* Volume 78, Number 3, May/June 2007.

Culbertson, F.M. (1957). Modification of emotionality held attitude through role playing J. *Abnorm. Soc. Psychol.,* 54.

David G. Perry., Kay Bussey and Judy Fischer (1980). Effects of rewarding children for resisting temptation on attitude change in the forbidden toy paradigm. In Australian *J.Psychol.*, Vol. 32. No. 3, 1980.

De Weiss, Pick., J. Susan, and A. David (1981). Problems in the administration of questionnaires with fixed response format and attitudinal scales in a developing country. Revista De La Association Latin Americana De Psychologica Social. Vol. 1 (1).

Dietrich J.E., (1946). The relative effectiveness of two modes of radio delivery in influencing attitudes. *Speech Monogr.,* 13.

Dietsch. R.W., and H. Gurnee (1948). Cumulative effect of a series of a campaign leaflets. *J. Apple. Psychol.,* 32.

Dillehay, R.C. C.A., Insko, and M.B. Smith (1966). Logical consistency and attitude change. *J. Pers. Soc. Psychol.,* 3.

Dittes J.E., and H.H. Kelley (1956). Effects of different conditions of acceptance upon conformity to group norms. *J. Abnorm. Soc. Psychol,* 53.

Dominique Brossard (2005). International journal of Science Education Volume 27. issue 9 July 2005.

Doob, L.W. (1940). Some factors determining change in attitude. *J. Abnorm. Soc. Psychol,* 35.

Dymkowaki. M. (1980). Self concept and attractiveness of source of perusal information. *Przeglad Psychologiozny*, 1980, Vol. 23(3).

Eagly A.H. and S. Chaiken (1975). An attribution analysis of the effect of communicator characteristics on opinion change: The case of communicator attractiveness. *J. Pers. Soc. Psychol.*, 32.

Eagly A.H., and R. Warrier (1976). Intelligence comprehension and opinion change. *J. Pers. Soc. Psychol.,* 44.

Eagly, A.H., and S.Chaiken (1976). Why would any one say that? Causal attribution of statements about the water gate scandal. Sociometry., 39.

Ebbesen E.B., W. Mishel, and A.R. Zeiss (1973). Selective attention to the self; situational and dispositional determinants. *Pers. Soc. Psychol.*, 27.

Eberhard, J.C. and R.A. Bauer (1941). An analysis of the influence eon recall of a controversial event. *J. Soc. Psychol.,* 14.

Edward. A.L., and F.P. Kilpatrick (1948). A technique for the construction of attitude scales. J. Appl. *Psychol.*, 32.

Edwards, A.L. & Porter, B.C. (1972). Attitude measurement. In The affective domain: A resource book for media specialists. Washington, DC: Gryphon House.

Eiser, J.R., and C.J. Mowerwhite (1969). The persuasiveness of labels: Attitude change produced through definition of the attitude change continuum. *Eur. J. Soc. Psychol.,* 4.

Ekman, P.A. (1958). A comparison of verbal and non-verbal behaviour as reinforcing stimuli of opinion responses. Doctoral dissertation. Adephi. Univ.

Eldersveld. S.J. (1956). Experimental propaganda techniques and voting behavior. *Amer. Polit. Soi. Rev.*, 50.

Etaugh, C. (1982). Changes in attitude towards women, College students – 2 year longitudinal study. *Psychol. Abst.*, Vol. 67. No. 6. Part 2, Index Jan-June, 82.

Evans R.I., P.M. Rozelle, R. Noblit, and D.L. Williams (1975). Explicit and implicit persuasive communications over time to initiate and maintain behavior change: New perspectives utilizing real – life dental hygiene situation. *J. App. Soc. Psychol.*, 5.

Farakas, A.J., and N.H. Anderson (1976). Integration theory and inoculation theory as explanation of the 'paper-tiger' effect. *J. Soc. Psychol.*, 98.

Festinger L., and J.M. Carlsmith (1959). Cognitive consequence of forced compliance. *J. Abnorm. Soc. Psychol.*, 58.

Festinger. L and J. Thibant (1951). Intrapersonal communicational in small groups. *J. Abnorm. Soc. Psychol.*, 46.

Festinger, L. (1957). A Theory of Cognitive Dissonance. Stanford: Standford Univ. Press.

Fine, B.J. (1957). Conclusion – Drawing, communicator credibility and anxiety as factors in opinion change. *J. Abnorm. Soc. Psychol.*, 54.

Fishbein, M. (1963). An investigation of the relationships between beliefs about an object and attitude toward that object. *Hum. Relat.*, 16.

Fisher, S., I. Rubinstein, and R.W. Freeman (1956). Intertrial effects of immediate self committal in a continuous social influence situation. *J. Abnorm. Soc. Psychol.*, 52.

Freedman, J.L (1965). Long -Term behavioral effects of cognitive dissonance. *J. Exp. Soc. Psychol.*, I.

Freedman, J.L. (1963). Attitudinal effects of inadequate Justification. *J. Abnorm. Soc. Psychol.*, 69.

French, J.R.P., Jr. and R. Snyder (1959). Leadership and interpersonal power. In D. Cartwright (Ed.). Studies in Social Power. Ann Arbor., Univ of Michigan Press.

Garrette, H.e., fand R.S. Woodworth (1958). Statistics in Psychology and Education. Longmans, Green and Co., INC.

Gelfand, D.M. (1962). The influence of self-esteem on the rate of verbal conditioning and social matching behavior. *J. Abnorm. Soc. Psychol.*, 65.

Gerard H.B. (1953). The effect of different dimensions of disagreement on the communication process in small groups. *Hum. Relst.*, 6.

Gerard H.B., E.S. Conolley, and R.A. Wilhemy (1974). Compliance, justification and cognitive change. Adv. Exp. Soc. Psychol., 7.

Gewirtz, J.L., and D.M. Baer (1958). Effects of brief social deprivation on behavior for a social reinforce. *J. Abnorm. Soc. Psychol.*, 56.

Goldberg S.C. (1954). Three situational determinants of conformity to social norms. J. Abnorm. Soc. Psychol., 49.

Gollob. H.F. and J.E. Dittes (1965). Different effects of manipulated self-esteem on persuasibility depending on the threat and complexity of the communication. *J. Pers. Soc. Psychol.* 30.

Green A.L., H.J.S. Sullivan, and B.T. Karen (1982). Attitudinal effects of the use of role models in information about sex – typed careers. (Arizona State Univ). *J. Educ. Psychol.*, Vol. 74(3).

Green, D. (1974). Dissonance and self – perception analyses of 'forced – compliance' – when two theories make competing predictions. *J. Pers. Soc. Psychol.*, 29.

Greenbaum C.W. (1963). The effect of choice and reinforcement on attitude change in a role – playing situation. Doctoral dissertation, New York. Univ.

Greenstein, F. (1965). Children and Politics. New Haven: Yale Univ. Press.

Greenwald. H.J. (1959). Dissonance and relative vs absolute attractiveness of decision alternatives. *J. Pers. Soc. Psychol.*, 11.

Griffin, K., and L. Ehrlich (1963). Attitudinal effects of a group discussion on a proposed change in company policy. *Speech Monogr.*, 30.

Gruner, C.R. (1965). An experimental study of satire as persuasion. *Speech Monogr.*, 32.

Guilford, J.P. (1959). Personality. New York: Mc New will.

Gulley. H.E, and D.K. Berlo (1956). Effect of intercellular and intra-cellular speech structure on attitude change and learning. *Speech Monogr.*, 23.

Gulliksen. H. (1950). Theory of Mental Tests. John Wiley; New York.

Gultman, L. (1950). The problem of attitude and opinion management, in S.A. Stoffer (Ed). Measurement and Pre Direction Princeton: Princeton Uni. Press.

Hadley, H.D. (1953). The non-directive approach in advertising appeals. *J. Appl. Psychol.*, 37.

Haefner, D.P. (1956). Some effects of guilt arousing and persuasions and opinion change. Doctoral disseratation. *Univ. of Rochester.*

Haire, M. (1950). Human Relations, 3.

Haire, M.and F.Morrison (1957). School childern's perception of labour management, 3, 403-412. *J. Soc. Psychol.*, 46.

Hall. W. (1938). The effect of defined social stimulus material upon the stability of attitudes toward labour unions, capital punishment. social insurance and Negroes. *Purdue Univ. Stud.. Higher Educ.*, No. 7-19.

Hamond K.R. (1948). Measuring attitudes by error – choice: an indirect method. *J. Abnorm. Soc. Psychol.*, 43.

Hartman G.W. (1936). A field experiment on the comparative effectiveness of emotional and rational political leaf lets in determining election results. *J. Abnorm. Soc. Psychol.*, 31.

Harvey O.J. (1962). Personality factors in resolution of conceptual incongruities. Sociometry, 25.

Harwood, K. (1951). An experimental comparison of listening comprehension with reading comprehension. Speech Monogr., 18.

Hass, R.G. and K. Grady (1975). Temporal delay, type of forewarning and resistance to influence. *J. Pers. Soc. Psychol.*, 11.

Haugh, O. (1952).The relative effectiveness of reading and listening to radio drama as ways of imparting information and shift of attitudes. *J. Educ. Res.*, 45.

Hendrick, C., and M. Giesen (1976). Self attribution of attitude as a function of belief feedback. *Mem Cognit.*, 4.

Hess, E.H., (1965). Attitude and pupil size. *Sci Amer.*, 212.

Hildum, D.C., and R.W. Brown (1956). Verbal reinforcement and interviewer bias. *J. Abnorm. Soc. Psychol.*, 53.

Hilgard E.R. (1965). Hypnotic Susceptibility. New York; Harcourt, Brace, and world.

Himmelfarb, S. (1974). (Ed.) "Resistance" to persuasion induced by information – integration. In Reading in Attitude Change..

Himmelfarb, S., and D. Arazi (1974). Choice of source attractiveness in exposure to discrepant messages, *J. Exp. Soc. Psychol.*, 10.

Himmelfarb. S., and N.H. Anderson (1975). Integration theory applied to opinion attribution. *J. Pers. Soc. Psychol.* 31.

Hochbaum, M.L. (1954). Some psychodynamic factors in compulsive conformity. *J. Pers. Soc. Psychol.*,48.

Horowitz, M., J. Lyons, and H.V. Perl mutter. (1951). Induction of forces in discussion groups. HUM. RELAT, 4.

Hovland C.I. and I.L. Janis and H.H. Kelley (1953). *Communication and Persuasion*, New Haven: Yale Univ. Press.

Hovland C.I. and M.J. Rosenberg, Eds. (1960). *Attitude Organization and Change*, New Haven: Yale Univ. Press.

Hovland, C.I. (1959). Reconciling conflicting results derived from experimental and survey studies of attitude change. *Amer, Psychologist*, 14.

Hovland, C.I. and I.L. Janis (Eds.) (1959). *Personality and Persuasibility.* New Haven: Yale Univ. Press.

Hovland, C.I. and W. Mandell (1952). An experimental comparison of conclusion – drawing by the communicator and by the audience. *J. Abnorm. Soc. Psychol.*, 47.

Hovland, C.I. and W. Weiss (1951). The influence of source credibility on communication effectiveness. Publ. Opin. Quart., 15.

Hoyland C.I., (Ed.,) (1957). *Order of Presentation in Persuasion.* New Haven: Yale Uni. Press.

Hoyland C.I., E.H. Campbell. And T. Brock (1957). The effect of 'commitment' on opinion change following communication. In C.IO. Hovland (Edf.,) *Order of Presentation in Persuasion.* New Haven: Yale Univ. Press.

Hull, C.L. (1933). Hypnosis *and Suggestibility.* New York: Appleton – Century.

Infante, D.A. (1975). Richness of fantasy and beliefs about attempts to refute a proposal as determinates of attitudes change. *Speech, Monogr.*, 42.

Insko C.A. (1965). Verbal reinforcement of attitude *J. Pers. Soc. Psychol.*, 2.

Insko, C.A. (1964). Primacy versus regency in persuasion as a function of the timing of arguments and measures. *J. Abnorm. Soc. Psychol.*, 69.

Insko, C.A. S. Worchel. R. Folger, and A. Kutkus (1975). A balance theory interpretation of dissonance. *PS. Rev.*, 82.

Insko, C.A., W. Turnbull and B. Yandell (1974). Facilities and inhibiting effects of distraction on attitude change. *Sociometry.*, 37.

Janet T. Spence, Eugene D. Hahn (1997). The Attitudes toward women scale and Attitude Change in college students Psychology of Women Quarterly 21 (1).

Janis I.L., A.A. Lumsdaine, and A.I. Gladstone (1951). Effects of pre-preparatory communication on reaction to subsequence newsevents. *Publ. Opin. Quart.*, 15.

Janis I.L., D. Kaye, and P. Krischner (1965). Facilitating effects of 'eating – while – reading' on responsiveness to persuasive communications. *J. Pers. Soc. Psychol.*, 1.

Janis J.L. (1954). Personality correlates of susceptibility to persuasion. *J.Pers.*, 22.

Janis, I.L and P.b. Field (1959). Sex differences and personality factors related to persuasibility. In C.I. Hovland and I.L. Janis (Eds.) *Personality and Persuability*. New Haven: Yale Univ. Press.

Janis, I.L. and S. Feshback (1953). Effect of fear arousing communication *J. Abnorm. Soc. Psychol.*, 48.

Janis, I.L., and B.T. King (1954). The influence of role playing an opinion change. *J. Abnorm. Soc. Psychol.*, 49.

Jansen, M.J., and L.A. Stolurow (1962). An experimental study in role playing. *Psychol.*Monogr., 76, No. 31.

Jastrebske. Ellen (1982). Experimenter's role and confederate reactions to counter – attitudinal description, post descriptive opinion realignment in forced – compliance paradigm. *Psychol. Abst.*, Vol. 67, No. 6, Part 2, Index Jan – Jun 82.

Johnson, N.F. (1968). Sequential verbal behavioiur. In V*eRBAL Behaviour and General Behaviour Theory*. Englewood Cliffs. Prentice Hall.

Kagan J., and H. Moss (1962). *From Birth to Maturity*. New York: Wiley.

Kahn. L.A. (1956). The organization of attitudes toward the Negor as a function of education. *Psychol.*Monogr. 65, No. 13 (Whole No. 330)

Kakker, S.B. (1970). Influence of teacher training on certain trainee's attitude. *Ind. Educ. Rev.* 5.

Kamal Bhutani (1977). A study of the effect of some cognitive and personality factors on attitude change. Ph.D. Thesis Abstract. J. *Educ. Res.*, 12(4).

Katz D. and E. Stotland (1959). A preliminary statement of a theory of attitude structure and change. In S. Koch (Ed.,) *Psychology: Study of a Science*. Vol. 3, New York: McGraw-Hill.

Katz, D.I. Sarnoff, and C. Molintock (1956). Ego – defense and attitude change. *Hum. Relat*, 9.

Ketz. D. (1960). The functional approach to the study of attitude. *Publ. Opin. Quart.*, 24.

Kelly, E. (1955). Salience of membership and resistance to change of group norms where conformity is detrimental to group achievement. *Amer Social Rev.*, 19.

Kelman H.C. (1953). Attitude change as a function ion response restriction. *Hum. Relat.*, 6.

Kelman H.C. (1958). Compliance identification, and internalization: three processes of opinion change. *J. Confl. Fesol*, 2.

Kelman H.C. (1961). Processes of opinion change. *Publ. Opin.Quart.*, 25.

Kelman, H.C. (1950). Effects of success and failure on suggestibility in the auto kinetic situation. *J. Abnorm. Soc. Psychol.*, 45.

Kennedy, T.G. and R.A. Humphrey (1971). Effect of systems approach on changing per-service teacher attitude toward selected instructional design factors. *J. Educ.Res.*, 64.

Khatoon, T, and M.R. Verma (1982). A study f influence of personal factors on teacher's attitude towards job. *J. Inst. Educ.Res.*, Madras, 6, No. 2.

Kiesler, C.A. (1971). The psychology of commitment: Experimenters liking, behavior to belief., New York: Academic Press.

Kiesler, C.A., T.S. Roth, and M.S. Pallak (1974). Avoidance: reinterpretation of commitment and its applications. *J. Pers. Soc. Psychol.*, 30.

King. B.T. and I.L. Janis (1956). Comparison of the effectiveness of improvised versus non-improvised role–playing in producing opinion change. *Hum. Relat.*, 9.

Klingman, A. (1982). Persuasive communication in avoidance behavior: Using role stimulation as a strategy. Simulation and Games, Vol. 13 (1).

Knower, F.H. (1935). Experimental studies of change in attitudes: I. A study of the effect of oral arguments on change of attitudes. *J.Soc.Psychol.*, 7.

Knower. F.H. (1936). Experimental studies of change in attitudes: II. A study of the effect of printed arguments on changes in attitudes. *J. Abnorm. Soc. Psychol.*, 30.

Kraus, S., Ed. (1962). The Great Debate. Bloomington: Indiana Uni. Press.

Kretch, D., R.S. Crutchfield, and E.L. Ballachey (1962). *Individual in Society*. New York: Mc Graw – Hill.

Lana, R.E. and R.L. Rosnow (1963). Subject awareness and order effects in persuasive communications. *Psychol. Reports,* 12.

Lana. R.E. (1961). Familiarity and the order of presentation in persuasive communications. *J. Abnorm. Soc. Psychol.*, 62.

Langenbac, M. (1972). Development of an instrument to measure teacher's attitudes towards curriculum use and planning. *J. Educ.Res.*, 66(1).

Laventhal H., and S.I. Perloe (1962). A relationship between self – esteem and persuasibility. *J. Abnorm. Soc. Psychol.*, 64.

Laventhal, H., and J.C. Watts (1966). Sources of resistance to fear-arousing communications on smoking and lung cancer. *J. Pers.*, 34.

Laventhal, H., and P. Niles (1964). A field experiment on fear-arousal with data on the validity of questionnaire measures. *J. Pers.*, 32.

Laventhal, H., and P. Niles (1965). Persistence of Influence for varying durations of exposure to threat stimuli. *Psychol. Reports*, 16.

Laventhal, H., J.C. Watts, and F. Pagano (1967). Effects of fear and specificity of recommendation on smoking behaviour. New Haven: Department of Psychology, Yale Univ. (Mimeo).

Laventhal, H., Susan Jones, and G. Tembly (1966). Sex difference in attitude and behaviour change under conditions of fear and specific instructions. *J. Exp.Soc. Psychol.*, 2.

Laventhal. H. (1965). Fear communications in acceptance of preventive health practices. New Havent Dept. of Psychology, Yale Univ. (Mimeo).

Leeper M.R., D. Greene, R.E. Nisbett (1973). Undermining children's intrinsic interest with extrinsic reward: A test of the "Over Justification" hypothesis. *J. Pers. Soc. Psychol.*, 28.

Lependorf. S. (1964). The effects of incentive value and expectancy on dissonance resulting from attitude – discrepant behaviour and disconfirmation of expectancy. Doctoral dissertation, State University of New York, Buffalo.

Lepper, M.R. (1973). Dissonance self-perception and honesty in children. *J. Pers. Soc. Psychol.*, 25.

Lesser, G.S., and R.P. Ableson (1959). Personality correlates of persuasibility in children. In I.L. Janis. And C.I. Hovland (Eds.) *Personality and Persuability*. New Haven Yale Univ. Press.

Likert, R. (1932). A technique for the measurement of attitudes. *Arch. Psychol.* (N.Y.) No. 140.

Lindzey. G. and Aronson (1969). *The Hand Book of Social Psychology*. Addion Weslay, (2 Ed) (Vol. 3) Ch. 21. 'The nature of attitude and attitude change'.

London, H. (1973). Verbal and non-verbal expression of communicator's confidence. In *Psychology of the Peruafder*. Morristown, N.J.: General Learning.

Lull. P.E. (1940). The effectiveness of humour in persuasive speeches. *Speech Monogr.*, I.

Lumsdaine, A.A., and I.L.., Janis (1952). Resistance to counter – propaganda' produced by one – sided and two sided 'propagada' presentations. *Publ. Opin. Quart.*, 17.

Maier, N.R.F. and R.A. Maier (1957). An Experimental test of the effects of 'developmental' versus 'free' discussion on the quality of group decisions. *J. Appl. Psychol.*, 41.

Malof M and A.J., Lott (1962). Ethnocentrism and acceptance of Negro support in a group-pressure situation. *J. Abnorm. Soc. Psychol.*, 65.

Manefee, S.C. and A.G. Grannerberg (1940). Propaganda and opinios as foreign policy. *J.Soc. Psychol.*, 11.

Martin, B.L. & Briggs, L.J. (1986). The cognitive and affective domains: Integration for instruction and research. Englewood Cliffs, NJ: Educational Technology Publications.

Mathews J. (1947). The effects of loaded language on audience comprehension of speeches. *Speech Monogr.,* 14.

Mausner, B., and J. Mausner (1955). A study of anti-scientific attitude. *SI. Amer.*, 1992, No. 2.

Mausner. B. (1954). Studies in social interaction: III. Effects of variation in one partner's prestige on the interaction of observe pairs. *J. Appl. Psychol*, 37.

Mazer. G.E. (1969). Ballots and broadcasts, exposure to election broadcasts and terminal voting decisions. *Publ. Psychol., Quart.*, 3.

Mc Bride, D. (1954). The effects of public and private change of opinion on inter group communication. Doctoral dissertation, University of Minnesota.

Mc Garvey, H.R. (1943). Anchoring effects in absolute judgment of verbal material. *Arch. Psychol.*, 1943, No. 281.

Mc Guire, W.J. (1957). Order of presentation as a factors in 'conditioning' persuasiveness. In C.I. Hovland (Ed.) *Order of Resentation in Persuasion.* New Haven: Yale Univ. Press.

Mc Guire, W.J. (1964). Attitudes and opinions. *Annual Rev. Psychol.*, 17.

Mc Guire, W.J. (1968). The nature of attitude and attitude change. In the Handbook of Social Psychology. G. Lindzey and Aronson (Eds.), Vol. 3, Amerind Pub. Co., 21.

Mc Guire, W.J. and D. Papageorgis (1961). The relative efficacy on various types of prior belief – defense in producing immunity against persuasion. *J. Abnorm. Soc. Psychol.*, 62.

Mc Guire. W.J. (1961). Effects of serial position and proximity to 'reward' within a demonstration film. In A.A. Lumsdaine (Ed.) *Students Response in Programmed Instruction.* Washington, D.C.: National Academy of Science.

Mc Guire. W.J., (1960). A syllogistic analysis of cognitive relationships. In C.I. Hovlands and M.J. Rosenberg (Eds.) *Attitude Organization and Change.* New Haven: Yale Univ. Press.

Mc Keachie, W.J. (1954). Individual conformity to the attitudes of classroom groups. *J. Abnorm. Soc. Psychol.*, 49.

Mc Killip, J. (1975). Credibility and impression formation. *Per. Soc. Psychol.Bull.*, 1.

Mc Killip, J. and J.D. Edwards (1975). Source characteristic and attitude change. *Per.Soc. Psychol.Bull.*, 1.

Mc Kinnon, David H.; Nolan, C. J. Patrick; Sinclair, Kenneth E. (2000). A Longitudinal Study of Student Attitudes toward Computers: Resolving an Attitude Decay Paradox, Journal of Research on Computing in Education.

Mc Luhan, M. (1964). *Understanding Media.* New York: Mograw Hill.

Mc Luhan, M. and Q. Fiore (1967). *The Medium is the Message.* New York: Bantam.

Mc Peek, R.W and A.E. Gross (1975). Evolutions of presidential campaign speakers as functions of similarity and expectancy disconfirmations. *J.App.Soc. Psychol,* 5.

Mc Peek, R.W. and J.D. Edwards (1975). Expectancy disconfirmation and attitude change. *J. Soc. Psychol,* 96.

McDonald, F. & Kielsmeier, C. (1972). Social learning theory and the design of instructional systems. In The affective domain: A resource book for media specialists, Washington, DC: Gryphon House.

McKinnon, David H.; Nolan, C. J. Patrick; Sinclair, Kenneth E. (2000). A Longitudinal Study of Student Attitudes toward Computers: Resolving an Attitude Decay Paradox, Journal of Research on Computing in Education.

Mead, G.H. (1934). Mind, Self and Society. Chicago: Univ. of Chicago press.

Merton, R.K. (1957). *Social Theory and Social Structure.* Glencol., Ill. Free Press.

Messerschmidt R. (1933). The suggestibility of boys and girls between ages of six and sixteen years. *J. Genet. Psychol.,* 43.

Milgam. S. (1963). Behavioral study of obedience. *J. Abnorm. Soc. Psychol.,* 67.

Milgram. S. (1964). Group pressure and action against a person. *J. Abnorm. Soc. Psychol.,* 69.

Milgram. S. (1974). Obedience to Authority: An Experimental View. New York. Harper and Row.

Miller G.R. and M.A. Hewgill (1966). Some recent research on fear -- arousing message appeals. *Speech Monogr.* 33.

Miller G.R., and M.A. Hewgill (1964). An experimental study of the relationships of fear appeals, source credibility and attitude change. East Lansing: Department of communication, Michigan State University (Mimeo).

Miller N., and D.T. Campbell (1959). Recency and primary in persuasion as a function of the timing of speeches and measurement. *J. Abnorm. Soc. Psychol.,* 59.

Miller N., G. Maruyama, R.J., Beaber and K. Valone (1976). Speed of speech and persuasion. *J. Soc. Psychol.,* 34.

Miller, G.R., and M.A. Hewgill (1964). The effects of Variations in nonfluency on audience ratings of source credibility. *Quart. J. Speech,* 50.

Mullis, R.L., and D.M. Bornhoeft (1982). Children's attitudes to television advertisements: A factorial perspective. *J. Psychol.,* 113.

Munson, P., and C.A. Kiesler (1974). The role of attributions by others in the acceptances of persuasive communications. *J. Pers.,* 42.

Murphy. G., and L.B. Murphy. And T.N. Newcomb (1937). Experimental social psychology (Rev. Ed.) New York. Harper.

Nayar, P.R. (1975). A study of the attitudinal and proficiency changes sought to be achieved through perseveres teacher educations. *Late. Jub. Conf.* Mysore, Dec., 1975.

Nemeth C., and J. Edicott (1976). The midpoint as an anchor: Another look at discrepancy of position and attitude change. Sociometry, 39.

Newcomb T.M (1943). Personality and Social Change. New YorkL: Dryden.

Newcomb, T.M. (1961). The Acquaintance Process. New York: Holt, Rinehart,and Winston.

Nunnally, J.C. (Jr.) (1970). Introduction to psychological measurement. Int. Stu. Ed. McGraw-Hill.

Nuttin J.M, (1968). Attitude change after rewarded dissonant and consonant "forced compliance." Interen, *J. Psychol.*, 1.

Osgood. J.M. (1962). Studies on the generality of affective meaning system. Amer. Psychologist, 17.

Ostrom, T.M., C.M. Stele. And J. Simlanaky (1974). Perceived discrepancy and attitude change. An unsubstantiated relationship. *Rep. Res. Soc. Psychol.*, 5.

Pallak M.S. S.E. Sogin, and A Van Zante (1974). Bad decisions. Effect of volition, locus of causality and negative consequence on attitude change. *J. Pers. Soc. Psychol.*, 30.

Pareek, U., and T.V. Rao (1982). Development Motivation thorugh experiencing. New Delhi: Oxford & IBH Pub., Co.

Paulson, S.F. (1954). The effects of prestige of the speaker and acknowledgement of opposing arguments ion audience retention and shift of opinion. *Speech Monogr.* 21.

Payne. R. (1955). Attitude of the high school students in rural and urban areas of Georgia toward their wives working after marriage. Unpublished Papers, Department of Sociology.

Peak. Helen (1955). Attitude and motivation. In M.R. Jones (Ed.) *Nebraska Symposium on Motivation*, 1955. Lincoln: Univ. of Nebraska Press, Motivation, 1955. Lincoln: Univ. of Nebraska Press.

Peck, R.F. and R.J. Havighurst (1960). The Psychology of Character Development. New York. Wiley.

Pennington. D.F.F. Hararey and B.M. Bass (1958). Some effects of decision and discussion on coalescence. Change, effectiveness. *J. Appl.* Psychol., 42.

Perry, D.G. K. Bussey and J. Fischer (1980). Effects of potion pictures on the social attitudes of high school children. Chicago: Univ. of Chicago press.

2Peterson, Christopher; Seligman, Martin E.; Vaillant, George E (1988). AIDS and Homosexuality: A Longitudinal Study of Knowledge and Attitude Change Among Rural Nurses, Journal of Personality and Social Psychology.

Peterson, R.C. and L.L. Thrustone (1933). The effect of motion pictures on the social attitudes of high school children. Chicago: Univ. of Chicago Press.

Petty. R.C., J.T. Cacioppo, and G. Rachel (1981). Personal involvement as a determinant of argument based persuasion. Pers. Sos. Psychol., 1981 (Nov.) Vol. 41(5).

Powell, F.A (1965). Source Credibility and behavioral compliances as determinates of attitude change *J. Pers. Soc. Psychol.*, 2.

Prawat, Richard S (1979). Longitudinal Study of Attitude Development in Pre-, Early, and Later Adolescent Samples, Journal of Educational Psychology.

Rao. P.S. (1984). Changing Certain Attitudes in Urban Secondary School students – A study of Teaching Techniques and Effects, Ph.D. thesis submitted to the University of Mysore.

Raven, B.H., and J.R.P. French (1958). Legitimate power, coercive power, and observability in social influence. Sociometry, 21.

Reddy, .V.R. (1981). A study of the attitude toward internal assessment. *J. Educ. Res..*, Madras Vol. 5, No. 2, May 1981.

Reiss, M., and B.R. Schlenker (1977). Attitude change and responsibility avoidance as methods of dilemma resolutions in forced compliance situations. *J. Pers. Soc. Psychol.*, 35.

Remmers H.H. R.E. Horton, and S. Lysgard (1952). Teenage personality in our culture – The purdue opinion poll report No. 32. Lafayett, and; Purdue Univ. Studies. Purdue Univ.

Richardson, G.A. (1981). Student – teacher attitudes toward decision – making in schools before and after taking up their first appointments. *Educational Studies*, 1981, Vol. 7(1).

Robbins, P.R. (1962). Self-reports on reaction fear arousing" information. *Psychol.* Reports. 11.

Rosenberg, M.J. (1965). An analysis of affective – cognitive consistency. In Hovland and M.J. Rosenberg (Eds.) Attitude Organization and Change. New Haven: Yale Univ. Press.

Rosenthal R.L. (1967). Covert communication in the psychological. Learning Strategies. Experiment. Psychol. Bull., 67.

Ross, L., G. Bierbruer, and S. Hoffman (1976). Causal inferences about communicators and their effect on opinion change. Presented at Annual meet East Psy. Association, Boston (48).

Ross, M., and R.F. Shulman (1973). Increasing the salience of initial attitudes: Dissonance vs self-perception theory. *J. Pers. Soc. Psychol.*, 28.

Rowley,V.and F.D.Keller(1962).Changes in childern's verbal behaviour as a function of social approval and manifest aniexiety. *J. Abnorm. Soc. Psychol.*, 65.

Sainsbury, M. & Schagen, I. (2004). Attitudes towards reading at ages nine to eleven. Journal of Research in Reading, 27.

Sampson, E.E., and C.A. Insko (1964). Cognative consistency and conformity in autokinetic situvtation. *J. Pers. Soc. Psychol.*, 55.

Scott, W.A. (1957). Attitude change through reward of verbal behavior. *J.Abnorm. Soc. Psychol.*, 55.

Scott. O. and S.C. Brinskly (1960). Attitude change of student – teachers and validity of MTAL. Theory in Education. *J. Educ. Psychol.*.51, Apr. 1960.

Shaffer D.R. (1974). Attitude extremity as a determinant of attitude change in the forced – compliance experiment. *Bull. Psychol.. Soc.*, 3.

Shaffer, D.R. (1975). Some effects of consonant and dissonant advocacy on initial attitude. Salience and attitude change. *J. Pers. Soc. Psychol.*, 32.

Shallenberger, P., and E. Zigler (1961). Rigidity, negative reaction tendencies and coastation effects in normal and feebleminded children. *J. Abnorm. Soc. Psychol.*, 2.

Shankar, P. (1982). Prediction of attitude not behaviour. First approximation. *Psychol. Rep.*, 1982 (Apr.) Vol. 50(2).

Sherif. C.W. and M. Sherif (Eds.) (1967). Attitude, Ego. Involvement and Change. New York: Wiley.

Sherif. M. and C.I. Hovland (1961). Social Judgement. New Haven. Yale Univ. Press.

Sheriff. M. (1935). A Study of some social factors in perception. Arch. *Psychol.*,. (N.Y.) No. 187.

Sherwood, J.J. (1965). Self-identity and referent others. Sociometry, 28.

Shouksmith, G. (1983). Change in attitude to retirement following a short preretirement planning seminar. Massey Univ. New Zealand.

Shrauger, J.S. (1975). Responses to evaluation as a function of initial self perceptions. *Psychol.*, Bull, 82.

Silverman I. (1964). Differential effects of ego threat upôn persuasibility for high and low-esteem subjects. *J. Abnorm. Soc. Psychol.*, 69.

Silverman, I., L.H. Ford, and J.B. Morganti (1966). Interrelated effects of social desirability, sex, self-esteem and complexity of argument ion persuasibility. *J. Pers.*, 34.

Silverthrone, C.P. and L. Mazmanian (1975).The effects of heckling and media of presentation on the impact of a persuasive communication. *J. Soc. Psychol.*, 96.

Simonson, M. and Maushak, N. (2001). Instructional technology and attitude change. In D. Jonassen (Ed.), Handbook of research for educational communications and technology. Mahway, NJ: Lawrence Erlbaum Associates.

Simonson, M.R. (1977). Attitude change and achievement: Dissonance theory in education. *J. Educ. Res.*, 70(3), Jan, Feb, 1977.

Sims, V.M. (1938). Factors influencing attitude toward the TVA. *J. Abnorm. Soc. Psychol.*, 33.

Singh and Sharma (1976). Teaching attitude as a determinant for classroom verbal interaction. *J. Educ. Res.*, 1 (1) Jan, 1976.

Singh. R.A and S.K. Saxena (1981). Agra Psycology Research Cell (APRC) Tiwari Kothi, Belananj – 282004 (India), Agra – 4 Copyright 1981.

Singh, A.J. (1979). Indian norms of the *Mtai. Ind. Educ. Rev.* Vol. XIV. No. 4.

Sinha, A.K.P. and O.P. Upadhyaya (1960). The persistence in the stereotypes of university students toward different athnic groups during sino-indian boarder dispute. *J.Soc. Psychol.*, 52.

Smith E.E. (1961). The power of dissonance techniques to change attitudes. *Publ. Opin. Quart.*, 25.

Smith, P. & Ragan, T.J. (1999). Instructional design. New York: John Wiley & Sons.

Smith, Mickey et. al (1991)Smith. M.B. J.S. Bruner, and R.W. White (1956). *Opinions and Personality*. New York: Wiley.

Snider M. (1962). The relation between fear arousal and attitude change. *Diss. Abs.*, 23.

Srivatsava, N (1981). A scale to measure teacher's attitude toward population education in secondary schools. DFTE. Univ. of Lucknow. *Ind. Educ. Rev.*, Vol. 14, No. 4.

Srivatsava. N. and D.A. Tiwari (1979). Study of the attitude of secondary school teachers during and after emergency period toward the need of population education. *J. Educ. and Psychol.* 37(2).

Staats A.M. and C.K. Staats (1958). Attitudes established by classical conditioning *J. Abnorm. Soc. Psychol.*, 57.

Stanley. J.C. and H.J. Klausmeier (1957). Opinion constancy after formal role playing. *J. Soc. Psychol.*, 46.

Stephenson, W. (1953). A study of behavior: Q-Technique and its Methodology. Chicago: Univ. of charge press.

Stevenson, H.W. R. Kean, and R.M. Knights (1963). Parents and strangers as reinforcing agents for children's performance. *J. Abnorm. Soc. Psychol.*, 67.

Stone. C.P., and R.G. Barker (1950). The attitudes and interests of premenar – ehical and post monarchical girls. *J. Genetic. Psychol.* 41.

Stotland E., and M. Patchen (1961). Identification and changes in prejudice and in authoritarianism. *J. Abnorm. Soc. Psychol.*, 62.

Stotland E., D. Katz, and M. Patchen (1959). The reduction of interpersonal similarity. *J. Abnorm. Soc. Psychol.*, 2, pp. 250-256.

Stotland, E. and R. Dunn (1962). Identification 'Oppositeness' Authoritarianism, Self–esteem and birth order, *Speech . Monogr*, 76, No. 9 (Whole No. 528).

Stroebe, Wolfgang, and D. Michael (1981). conformity and action of interpersonal behavior. The Effect of social support an attitude change. *J. Pers. Soc. Psychol.*, 41(5).

Stromer, W. (1954). An investigation into some of the relations between reading listenin and intelligence *Speech . Monogr.*

Stukat, K.G. (1958). Suggestibility: A Factorial and Experimental Study. Stockholm: Almgvist and Wiksell.

Susana d Souza Barros and Marcos F. Elia (1998). "Physics teacher's attitudes: how do they affect the reality of the classroom and models for change?" from: Connecting Research in Physics Education with Teacher Education, An I.C.P.E. © Book International Commission, on Physics Education 1997,1998, Federal University of Rio Dejaneiro, Brazil.

Taylor; S.E (1952). communications "Prophets" are they any good *Journalism Quart,* 29.

Taylor, S.E. (1975). On inferring one's attitude from one's behavior: some limiting conditions. *J. Pers. Soc. Psychol.* 31.

Te deshi.J.T.B.R. Schlenkar. And T.V. Bonona (1971). cognitive dissonance: Private nationalization or public Spectacle? *Amer Psychol* . 26.

Thrasker, J. (1954). Interpersonal relations and gradations of stimulus structure as factors in judgmental variations: an experimental approach. *J.Soc. Psychol*. 9.

Thrustone. L.L. (1929). *The Measurement of Social Altitudes*. Chicago: Univ. of Chicago Press.

Thrustone. L.N. and E.J. Chave (1929). *The Measurement of Attitudes.* Chicago: Univ. of Chicago Press.

Thuthill, D.M. and D.R. Forysth (1982). Sex differences in opinion conformity and dissent. *J. Soc. Psychol.* 1982 (Apr.) Vol. 116(2).

Toussaint. I.H. (1960). A classified summary of listening, 1950- 1959. *J. Communic.*, 10.

Traineds, H.C. (1971). Attitude and Attitude change, USA. John Wiley.

Tuckman, B.W. (1972). *Conducting Educational Research.* U.S.A. : Harcourt Brace Javanovich Inc. (1972, 78).

Tuna, E., and N. Livson (1960). Family, SES and Adolescent attitude toward authority. *Child Development*, 31.

Tuthill, D.M., and D.R. Forysth (1982). Sex differences in opinion conformity and dissent. *J. Soc. Psychol.*, 1982 (Apr.), Vol. (2), pp. 205-210.

Twist, L., Gnaldi, M., Schagen, I. & Morrison, J. (2004). Good readers but at a cost? Attitudes towards reading in England. Journal of Research in Reading, 27.

Tylor. W.L. (1952). Communication 'prophets': Are they good? *Journalism Quart.* 29.

Uzunboylu, Huseyin (2007). Teacher attitudes toward online education following an online inservice program, International Journal on E-Learning, Sunday, April 1, 2007.

Vellaisamy, M (2007). Effectiveness of Multimedia approach in Teaching Science at Upper Primary level, Indian Educational Review, Vol. No.43, Nov. 1st, Jan. 2007.

Verma (1982). A study f influence of personal factors on teacher's attitude towards job. *J. Inst. Educ.Res.*, Madras, 6, No. 2.

Wallach, M.A. N. Kogan, and D.J. Bem (1962). Group Influence on individual risk taking. *J. Abnorm. Soc. Psychol.*, 65.

Wang. K.A. (1932). Suggested criteria for writing attitude statements. *J. Soc. Psychol.*, 3.

Watts W.A., and W.J., Mc Guire (1964). Persistence of induced opinion change and retention of inducing message content. *J. Abnorm. Soc. Psychol.*, 68.

Watts. W.A. (1967). Relative persistence of opinion chage induced by active compared to passive participation. *J. Pers. Soc. Psychol.*, 5.

Weiss W. (1957). Opinion congruence with negative source on one issue as a factor influencing agreement on another issue. *J. Abnorm. Soc. Psychol.*, 54.

Weiss, R.F. (1960). Emotional arousal and attitude change. *Psychol Reports.*, 6.

Weiss, W., and B.J. Fine (1955). Opinion change as a function of some interpersonal attributes of the communicates. *J. Abnorm. Soc. Psychol.*, 51.

Weiss. R.F. N.E. Rawson and Pasamanick (1963). Argument strength, delay of argument and anxiety in the conditioning and selective learning of attitudes. *J. Abnorm. Soc. Psychol.*, 67.

Weitzenhoffer. A.M. (1953). Hypnotism: An Objective Study In Suggestibility. New York: Wiley.

Wetzel, C.D., Radtke, P.H. & Stern, H.W. (1994). Instructional effectiveness of video media. Hillsdale, NJ: Lawrence Erlbaum Associates.

Wicklund. R.A. and (1974). *Freedom and Reaction.* Potomac, Md., Earlbaum.

Williams, E. (1975). Medium or message: communications medium as a determinant of interpersonal evaluations. *Sociometry.*, 38.

Windies. R.R. (1961). A comparison of listening and reading as means of testing of *J.Educ.Res.,* 52.

Wittaker. J.C and R.d. Meade (1967). Sex of the communicator as a variable in source credibility. J. Soc. Psychol.,72.

Wood, W., A.H. Eagly, and S. Chaiken (1977). Causal influences about communicators and their effect on opinion change presented at annual meet. East pay. Association, Boston (48).

Worchel S. and S.E. Arnold (1974). The effect of combined arousal states on attitude change. *J. Exp. Soc. Psychol.*, 10.

Worchel S. S. Arnold and M. Baker (1975). The effect of sensorship on attitude change. The influence of censor and communication characteristics. *J. Appl. Soc. Psychol.*, 5.

Wyers. R.S. (Jr.) (1974). Cognitive organization and change -- an information processing approach. Potomac. Md.: Erlbaum.

Yeshodhara. K. (1979). A study of some attitudinal and proficiency changes achieved through teacher education. Ph.D. Thesis, Univ. of Mysore.

Young, J. (1953). An experimental comparison of vocabulary growth by means of oral reading silent reading and listening. *Speech Monogr.*. 20.

Zagonc, R.B. (1960). The progress of cognitive tuning in communication. *J. Abnorm. Soc. Psychol.*, 61.

Zanna, M.P. E.T. Higgins, and P.A. Taves (1976). Is dissonance phenomenological aversive. *J. Abnorm. Soc. Psychol.*,12.

Zanna. M.P. J.M. Olson and R.H. Fazio (1980). Attitude behavior consistency. An individual difference perspective. *J. Pers. Soc. Psychol.*, 38.

Zimbardo, P.G. & Leippe, M.R. (1991). The psychology of attitude change and social influence . New York: McGraw-Hill.

Zimbardo. P.G. (1960). Involvement and communication discrepancy as determinants of opinion conformity. *J. Abnorm. Soc. Psychol.*, 60.

Zimbardo. P.G. M. Weisenberge, I. Firestone and B. Levy (1965). Communicator effectiveness in producing public conformity and private attitude change. *J. Pers.*, 33.

—oo—